THE GOLFER'S CODE

A Guide To a Proper
and
Civilized Golf Game

THE GOLFER'S CODE

A Guide To a Proper
and
Civilized Golf Game

By David Gould
and the editors of *Golf Pro*

FAIRCHILD PUBLICATIONS
NEW YORK

Standard Book Number: 87005-741-3

Library of Congress Catalog Card Number: 92-76059

Printed in the United States of America

FOREWORD

Golf is a game, but it is a game that goes beyond the boundaries of simple recreation and carries us to the dark places of our own character. Into those dark places it shines a bright light so that we can see if we are honest, quick-tempered, mean-spirited, generous, courteous and other qualities that tell us who we are.

That is because golf, as played by most of us, has no umpire, no referee, no linesman. We are the officials and we call the penalties on ourselves. That is the one clean, fine thing that separates golf from other sports where duplicity is often a valuable stratagem.

In addition to this quality of self policing is a code of etiquette that we all learned at the same time we were trying to master the golf swing. And the etiquette was almost as important as knowing the rules. Things like who tees off first, where to stand on the tee and on the green, when to keep quiet, when to let a group play through and a bag of other common courtesies. The two elements of self policing and etiquette made golf a world of its own, an athletic Shangri-la where honesty and courtesy bloomed all year long.

But the great golfing boom of the last few decades has begun to erode those two hallmarks of the game. Thousands of people have taken up golf without being taught the rules or the etiquette of the sport. That has a two-fold effect. It makes the golf course a less pleasant place for those who care about such things and it deprives the new golfers of the complete enjoyment the game can afford.

So it is a very appropriate time for the editors of *Golf Pro* to have conceived and David Gould to have written *The Golfer's Code*. In it, he has set down all the things one can do to enjoy golf the proper way. He covers such mundane things as how to make up the proper foursome, how to arrange the proper wager on the first tee, how to correct a wayward partner or opponent. Mundane but important things.

He also breaks new ground in setting down for the first time in my experience the etiquette of the golf cart, which never crossed the minds of the founding fathers. What a great service this is, for if his advice is followed, those courses where carts are mandatory will see a marked speedup of play.

One of the joys of *The Golfer's Code* is that it can be used as a reference book or read straight through. It covers everything that surrounds the actual playing of the game.

The Golfer's Code should be required reading for every new golfer and many older ones. It can go a long way in refurbishing the honesty and courtesy that make golf something quite a part from other sports.

Jack Whitaker
Bridgehampton, N.Y.,
April 1993

PREFACE

Monday mornings, we often sit around the office at *Golf Pro* and talk about our previous weekend of golf. Scores are recited, holes recounted and swing flaws revealed. Throw in some conversation about the tour and we can kill a good 45 minutes at the beginning of each week.

On one particular Monday, an executive of our company started talking about his round at a private course where he was invited to play. But instead of complaints about another score in the 100's or why he still couldn't hit it longer than 200 yards, he was fixed on the rules. Not the written ones as we know them — but the unwritten ones. You know, where should he put on his shoes when he's a guest; what to pay a caddie; when to ask to play through. He wasn't sure of the proper way to handle some of these situations and wondered if there were a book he could read to guide him.

There wasn't. But by day's end we were in his office talking outlines, titles, structure, look, style, etc. *The Golfer's Code* was established.

Our strict mission in writing and publishing this book is to outline proper protocol for the multitude of situations that come up when a round of golf is planned, played and completed. It took months and months of dissecting thousands of rounds of golf to agree on the answers to all our questions. And still we will be the first to say we probably missed something. Which really is the beauty of the game and the reason for its perpetuity. Though deeply rooted in sacred traditions and customs, golf also changes with time. Fifty years ago, we wouldn't have had a chapter on carts and twenty years ago, there was no reason to address slow play.

It's our feeling that learning the unwritten codes of this book is just as important as learning how to swing. Golf is a lot more than just setting up, taking a grip, shifting your weight and following through. In fact, swinging the club accounts for about one hour of every four-hour round. That leaves a lot of time for social interaction.

More than anything, it's our hope this book will add to your enjoyment of the game. One golfer behaving awkwardly can turn a good time into a difficult one for all of us. To the extent that a bit of information can prevent such discomfort, we believe the relevant information should be gathered into the form of a book.

Acknowledgments

I am grateful to the president of Fairchild Publications, Michael Coady, Mark Sullivan, one of the publishers in his magazine group, and to Ken Cohen, this book's editor, for their patience and guidance during the past year. There is a certain presumptuousness in writing any book of manners and courtesy, and one needs continual reassurance and reorientation to keep up the discourse. I relied greatly on my collaborators, Ken Cohen particularly, for the feedback that allowed me to see both sides of the many decisions and judgments discussed in these chapters.

A debt of thanks is also owed to Pam Kirshen, who provided technical guidance and the sine qua non of modern publishing, a business plan. The book's design is the work of Edward Leida, and the use of the original Anthony Ravielli drawings of Bobby Jones was generously provided to us by the Chairman of the Board of Callaway Golf, Ely Callaway, Hartmarx — makers of the Bobby Jones line of apparel and the heirs of Bobby Jones.

We have dedicated this book to Bobby Jones, who in our opinion was the epitome of class and decorum on the golf course. He represented everything amateur golf should be and no book on the subject of proper protocol and behavior can be written without his spirit.

Lastly, to all the club members, golf professionals and old and new golfing friends whose invitations and urgings have landed me in enough foursomes and threesomes and twosomes to provide this book's requisite raw material, my heartfelt thanks. And heartfelt apologies for any breaches along the way; they were inadvertent.

David Gould
Sandy Hook, Connecticut
June 1993

Contents

THE GOLFER'S CODE

A Guide To a Proper
and
Civilized Golf Game

C H A P T E R

I

Your Game and My Game

*How a code of behavior reconciles
the differences*

It won't happen by the close of this century, but in a few decades American golf will have completed its changeover from an aristocratic to a democratic game. The option of playing golf will extend to virtually anyone who is interested. The ranks of top collegiate and professional players will represent a cross-section of society. And private clubs, never actually stripped of their constitutional right to admit whomever they wish, by degrees will have given up ethnic uniformity in favor of diversity for its own sake.

As this changeover runs its course, let's hope that American golf can retain the dignified and courtly qualities it may owe, in part, to its long years in the custody of the privileged classes. Can the inherent codes of the game, derived from its commoner-and-lord origins in 18th-century Scotland and nurtured by the country club system, be enough to preserve good manners?

1

The whispered vote of this little book is "aye." However, now that golf's playing fields are wide open, we find that our small peeves and preferences abound, threatening mutual happiness: You like to study course architecture, I like to bet. I play for stimulation, you're here to relax. You know the Rules, I make jokes about them. You walk, I ride. You drink, I don't. You give putts, I say make 'em. Fortunately, neither of us wants to call the whole thing off.

However, despite our best intentions to avoid irritating fellow golfers, our system for doing so is not what it could be. Everyone agrees that "proper golf etiquette" should be followed, but nowhere can we turn to find a comprehensive listing of exactly what is and what is not proper golf etiquette. The Rules of Golf, though an amazing and useful set of guidelines, do not venture much beyond the variables that affect score. For example, Rule 27-2 covers in detail the subject of the provisional ball. But nowhere does the rule suggest when it should be played. Immediately after the first attempt? When all other members of the group have played their tee shots? With a fuller consensus on questions such as this, golfing society will be more able to tolerate its normal diversity.

Another reason we should study the fine points of courtesy more closely is that modern golf is losing its natural tendency to engender humility. The equipment doesn't buzz our hands and jangle our elbow ligaments as it once did. The shoes don't weigh 68 pounds when they get wet. The balls don't suffer terminal injuries as a result of your two-degree change in spine angle during the swing. With less adversity, we are less prone to feel humble and part of the common suffering, more prone to turn inward in search of continual bliss.

The sentiment with the best chance of rallying all golfers to the cause of courtesy is one that is already current among us. That theme is expressed in the words: "Give something back to golf." Typically, this thought is associated with golf's institutionalized charities; it's a favorite closing line in letters from the chairmen of benefit tournaments. Sometimes a professional golfer will say these words in speaking about his or her visits with underprivileged children.

But indeed, no simpler means exist of giving something back to the game that has given you so much pleasure than to behave well on the course. In this regard, good intentions are nice, but they must be backed by a comprehensive understanding of how the social and competitive versions of the game unfold across the golf course. Only through understanding can a golfer be alert to all the situations that can affect group pleasure and harmony. What follows is a nearly complete catalogue of the game's many scenarios and situations, along with advice on how to handle them with grace and good sense.

CHAPTER

II

Tee to Fairway to Green

*Subtleties of golf etiquette:
the whole 6,500 yards*

What do you think would happen if four motorists set off together on an otherwise empty highway and were required to stay within a few car lengths of one another for an entire afternoon? However much they signaled for their lane changes and observed recommended spacing among themselves, they would most likely commit one or two noticeable breaches of road safety and etiquette along the way.

But not because any of the four was a scoundrel or a fiend. The vast majority of us enter a highway or a supermarket or some other public setting with honorable intentions regarding our personal behavior. We expect to go about our business harmlessly, interacting very little with other drivers or shoppers. At moments when our paths happen to cross, we are prepared to whisper "excuse me" and continue on. And this policy generally works.

But golf demands more. The golf course, as a setting, is so vastly superior to the highway or the supermarket or the train station that it calls upon us to behave in a manner that is more than tolerable, more than excuse-me-able. For once we have the leisure to think of others. For once we have an intricate ritual to fulfill. For once we have a physically beautiful environment and an atmosphere of serenity to help maintain. And, for once, we have a spectrum of human emotion — however contrived — to comprehend and respond to. In keeping with this rarified scene, we must be at our most generous and thoughtful.

As always, safety is the source of many of our courtesies. A round of golf is probably a more hazardous event than even the highway convoy described above. To experienced golfers, safety becomes so second nature that we forget just how many little movements and adjustments we make to prevent injury to ourselves or others.

Second only to safety precautions are the myriad subtle maneuvers we undertake to avoid snapping a fellow golfer's concentration and spoiling his or her stroke. And still more subtle are the actions and words we use to make our companions' trip around the course as free as possible from inconvenience and struggle. For example, focused on a difficult bunker shot, your companion walks long past the only rake in sight and prepares to play. She executes the shot, and realizes she has created a 40-yard backtrack for herself to fetch that far-off rake. If you are indeed responding to the spirit of the sport, you will be standing by with a rake you borrowed from the back bunker.

For the sake of one's own foursome as well those following, your journey should be as free as possible of zigzags and backtracking. In order to avoid unnecessary detours, you must take note of the cart signs, look ahead for bridges (on holes with brooks and streams), check the map on your scorecard for the course's routing (or watch the group ahead and follow their trail from each green to the next tee), anticipate the clubs you'll need and look around for dropped headcovers and other such items as you are leaving the spot you have just played from.

THE TEE

Most golfers observe the custom of honors on the tee. To start a round, honor is determined by lot. Typically, one player will flip a tee in the air and award first-tee honors to the player or team the tee points toward when it lands. A more definitive method is to have a player on Team A toss his ball to a Team B player, and have the Team B player call whether the number on the ball is odd or even. If the group has decided to play an individual game, such as Skins, they will often place four balls in a hat and draw for order of play. After one hole is played, the team or player with the honor retains it on the second tee if they have won or halved (tied) the first hole; they yield it if they have lost.

No matter how willing you are to play first when you have the honor or let others hit first when they do, merely deferring is not enough: you should know whose honor it is. Even if you are not keeping the card and even if you are acknowledged to be less the fiery competitor than your mates, the fact remains that no three people want to be asked the same obvious question 17 times in one day simply because your approach to golf is a relatively breezy one. Once each member of the group comprehends whose turn it is, the following considerations should be kept in mind:

➢ Relative to the path of approach to the general tee area, where are the tee markers? Are they pushed way back into a narrow chute of a tee box? If so, then all players will have to make quick decisions about where to place golf bags and/or park golf carts, where to stand so as to avoid injury and avoid causing distraction, and whether there is time to walk to the trash can or the ball washer. Staying alert to these logistical challenges will save you from making a misstep capable of irritating others. At convergences of more than one tee or green, it is particularly easy to block a cart path; whenever possible, leave space for another player or maintenance worker to drive past you.

➢ Spotting other player's shots off the tee is one of the most vital means you have of contributing to group happiness. In the rush to find a safe, unimpinging spot on a tee — particularly when the markers stretch across the entirety of the cleared and/or elevated land, and the natural waiting areas are amid shrubbery or on a precarious slope, or both — we often neglect to seek a good angle for spotting other players' shots. Wherever possible, however, the effort must be made. This is particularly true on holes that play into the glare of a setting sun.

➤ Especially on the tee of a par-3 hole, the thoughtful golfer will do his or her part to reconcile with reality the many and diverse distance markings on the scorecard, tee signage and sprinkler heads. This will speed club selection, if nothing else. (Keep in mind that distance markings on golf courses generally refer to the yardage from a given point to the center of the green.) Also, since par-3 holes tend to generate divots off the tee, there is an opportunity for some kind soul to scoop out a dose of top-dressing for the next player, or retrieve his divot, whichever is more practical.

➤ Since club selection applies similarly to all players on par-3 tees, the question arises as to whether we should always volunteer the number club that we have just hit. In groups where competition is relished and gamesmanship condoned, not reporting that you have hit a 6-iron, and hit it flush, is considered good behavior. In other company, to guard such information would be discourteous.

➤ Rule 27-2 allows a player to hit a provisional ball from the same spot whence he launched a ball that appears to have strayed out of bounds or become lost. The tee is the place where the invoking of Rule 27-2 is most often called for. Perhaps because the stroke-and-distance penalty for out-of-bounds and lost balls seems unfair to some golfers, the playing of provisional balls is often ignored and/or discouraged. "Oh boy. That could be deep in the hay," says a player who has just sliced his tee shot toward knee-high grass. "I better play a provisional."

"Come on, we'll find it," says his partner, eager to get to his own down-the-middle drive. Or worse:

"You can just drop a new ball when you get up there."

Whatever your opinion of Rule 27, it is an insult to deny someone else the right to adhere to it, provided he does so with good reason and without delay (and, to avoid further infractions, uses a ball of a different number, marking or brand). On first blush, it seems a harsh idea to penalize a player one stroke and then not permit him to drop a ball near the spot he feels his first one was lost or went out of bounds. But, if you think long and hard about how much less important a good driving game would become if the rule was relaxed, you'll see that it is well conceived. So, unless you are certain that no one in your regular group has any regard whatever for the Rules of Golf, you are obliged to hold your ground until everyone has hit their drives and is satisfied that no provisional tee balls need be played. When a provisional ball is played, it should be played immediately, if the player is ready.

➢ One final point, regarding distractions: For many golfers, a great big swing for an intended 240-yard shot is much more susceptible to concentration breaks than a little pass of the putter blade. However obvious a comment, then, we will repeat it here: Quiet on the tee, please.

BASICS TO REMEMBER

➤ Pick up your tee after you hit, unless it has flown many feet from impact.

➤ Be sure to identify your ball definitively. Two balls of the same brand, driven perfectly down the fairway and coming to rest next to each other, are considered by the Rules to be lost balls if they cannot be identified.

➤ If you rest clubs on the tee markers to avoid having their grips get wet, do so in a manner that does not usurp designated teeing area.

➤ Less skilled golfers who choose to play from tee markers that are forward of the ones their companions are using should be applauded for their pragmatism and their efforts to avoid slow play. Far from commending them, many back-tee golfers forget about the forward-tee users once they've hit their drives. For safety reasons, the entire foursome should proceed to the furthest-back tee, wait for all shots to be played from there, then move forward. This way, all players are able to track each drive that is played.

➤ Try to toss all broken tees into a trash can or into a pile next to one of the tee markers. This prevents damage to mower blades and helps preserve the turf.

DOWN THE FAIRWAY

Most slowdowns in play occur as a result of searches for stray shots. One nice thing about being an experienced golfer — even a relatively high-scoring one — is that you have greatly improved your ability to track errant shots and gauge where they may have landed. If you haven't, you should have.

Courtesy on the fairway is basically dependent upon your ability to find your own ball, help others find their balls, determine quickly how far you are from the green and be ready to play your shot when your turn comes. The sorriest sight in golf is four dolts searching endlessly for balls they neglected to track off the tee, then debating rancorously from their address positions as to who is away and should therefore play first. These same players regularly break the rule prohibiting anything more than a five-minute search for a lost ball.

If all involved would remember that honor on the fairway is, for a variety of reasons, less important and more flexible than honor on the greens and tees, our rounds would proceed with fewer delays. Be prepared to allow those closer to the hole than you to play before you do, and be prepared for them to offer you the same privilege.

Also be prepared for those moments when you and another player are ready at the same time and neither ball can rightly be judged further out than the other. What will probably ensue is a vaudevillian byplay along the lines of "After you," "No, after you," etc. A very few seconds of this will determine some order of play, so there is no call for irritation. At worst, you both hit at once. Some golfers do so as a matter of policy. Seldom, if ever, will their balls collide in mid-air.

There is, of course, a fine line between advancing promptly to your ball so as to be ready for your turn and walking dangerously and discourteously into the path of another player's shot. Whether or not you are in the potential path of another player's shot is difficult to define. Ironically, you can perhaps insult someone by keeping so far afield from their possible path as to suggest them capable of the miraculously errant shot. When in doubt, stay even with the player. The closer you get to the green, the less danger there is, since partial-force shots are much less likely to injure. At that point, there is more danger of distraction than injury.

These considerations cover safety and order of play within one's own group. As for the players ahead, little need be said other than: Don't play a shot that has any kind of chance to reach them. Downhill and downwind shots are especially tricky, with circumstances extending your shot beyond what you are otherwise capable of.

➤ As you walk past yardage plates in the fairway, look around to see who in your group might find the information relevant to their shot, and either report the yardage or be ready if they ask you. Remember that the 150-yard markers usually represent a point in the middle of the fairway that is 150 yards from the center of the green. Ironically, a bush along the rough that helps indicate 150 yards from the center of the green is, itself, slightly more or less than 150 yards out.

➤ If you've driven into another fairway, you face the task of safely playing your next shot in a way that will not slow either group — yours or the group on the other fairway. If you are fortunate, the other foursome will yield and allow you to make a shot. The process is complicated if one of their players has hit a very short drive and is looking to hit at about the same time you are. If your ball is out on the next fairway, but you couldn't play it promptly because there are players ahead of you (on your hole) for whom you must wait, you are best off jogging over to your ball, identifying it, then retreating to the side.

➤ In a foursome in which two players have missed the fairway by a lot, it's very possible to have all four players off searching and no evidence to the group behind that the hole isn't clear. Have enough presence of mind to leave a bag or a golf cart out where the group coming onto the tee can see it.

➤ As others in your group play their shots, make an effort to help them find their divots and replace them (except on Bermudagrass fairways, where divots are not cleanly cut and maintenance protocol is to fill the hole with sand from a bucket that may be mounted on your golf cart. When no sand mixture is available, don't replace a Bermudagrass divot, kick the surrounding turf inward with your toe. Similarly, be alert to help move an obstruction such as a rake, cart sign or set of ropes.

ON THE GREEN

The green is the most painstakingly-built portion of the course as well as the most expensive to maintain. It is where we make our most delicate shots and where we experience our most dramatic swings of fate. On the social side, each green serves as a rendezvous spot for the foursome. Whatever diaspora the party undergoes after leaving the tee, it can count on reconvening at the next putting surface.

It is on and around the green that our social behavior is under greatest scrutiny. We have an excellent opportunity there to either please or displease our fellow golfers. It is also around the green that the Rules are most precise and demanding. What follows is a list of guidelines for comportment on the putting surface, some of which are obvious, others, judging from general observation, must not be quite so apparent.

COURTESIES TO OBSERVE
AROUND THE GREEN

➢ Do not dig the ball out of the cup with your putter.

➢ Remember to return people's ball markers.

If your marker would interfere with another player's putt, follow this procedure: with the marker in place, align your putter blade with a fixed object (tree, post, bush) and move the mark in the direction of this object one or more lengths of the putter head. Move the marker. When replacing the ball, reverse the process. Remember the marker must go down on the original spot before the ball can be replaced.

➢ Avoid stepping on other people's lines, even if you are wearing sneakers or spike-less golf shoes.

➢ Don't straddle a putt. It isn't a breach of etiquette so much as a breach of the Rules; however, the infraction often does stem from our efforts to avoid stepping on others' lines.

➢ Cigars, cigarettes and soda cups may, if necessary, be placed on the green, but never so as to obstruct or distract. Golf bags may not be placed on the green.

➢ He furthest away plays first, including balls that are on the putting green but further from the hole than one or more balls that are not on the green. This, anyway, is the letter of the law. As custom has evolved, many golfers now yield their turn to allow players off the green to play on. This speeds play by insuring that the flagstick, once removed, will not be replaced until everyone in the group has holed out. In lieu of a caddie, the player with the shortest putt tends the pin.

➤ If you are walking (and carrying or wheeling your clubs), bring the clubs around to the spot on the green you would naturally cross in going directly to the next tee, then proceed with your putting. (Obviously, if doing so would block someone's route to the hole, adjust accordingly).

➤ Don't leave scrape marks by dragging your spikes. The Rules do not permit other players to repair these marks in the line of their putts. If you are new to the game, most likely your spikes are new, sharp and long, and you will be quite surprised by how easy it is to leave an angry scrape mark with them.

➤ Fix stray ball-marks you may find, as well as your own. Fixing a ball-mark is nothing more than lifting the turf upward with a tee or divot tool to remove the indentation.

➤ You may mark another player's ball for him or her, but it's best to do this in cases where the player in question is so far away he couldn't do so himself without holding up play. Don't make it into a specialty, because for the most part a player would rather mark his ball himself. It's part of most peoples' rituals and part of their preparation routines.

➤ When you tend the pin for someone, stand on the side of the hole away from where the curve of the green is taking the putt. Or, stand where your shadow will not fall across the line of the putt. Grasp the flag in your hand to keep it from flapping noisily. Remove the pin as soon as the player putts. Someone may have the pin tended when off the green, but it must be removed.

➤ You may hold the pin high above the hole for a player pitching from a deep bunker or some other spot below an elevated green. If you tend, you must remove the flagstick, otherwise if the putt hits the flagstick, the person who putted will be assessed a loss-of-hole penalty (in match play) or two-stroke penalty (in stroke play).

➤ During the several minutes that a foursome is on the green, one or more players will be surveying their putts while another player is actually putting. In order for play to proceed as quickly as possible, the player putting has to tolerate the movements of the other players. They, in turn, should cease moving and hold their positions at the time the player takes his stance to putt. Also, unless vast sums are riding on it, or it would cause you to step in another player's line, finish putting rather than mark and lift.

➤ When playing out-of-season in temperate climates, you can expect the course to have closed its regulation greens and set up temporary greens. Play to the temporary greens (using the automatic two-putt rule) and avoid walking on the permanent greens.

➤ After leaving the 9th green, make sure to take care of mid-round refreshment buying as quickly as possible. Stopping for lunch between nines will automatically lose you your place on the course.

SOME UNUSUAL SITUATIONS

➤ At times of the year when the greens are only marginally prepared to withstand player traffic, the course superintendent may cut two holes and have foursomes alternate use of them. Thus, if your group watches the group ahead putt out using a hole on the back left, you'll see that when they install the flagstick they'll be installing it in a hole on the right front. Your group plays to this front hole, then — unless you forget, which is fairly easy — you will install the flagstick in that hole on the back left. People who know and remember the little things like this are appreciated by fellow golfers and greens superintendents as well.

➤ When your ball lies on the edge of a section of green that scallops outward or swings away from the main body of the green — and when the hole is cut far from the center of the green — you may find that a small patch of fringe and/or rough lies between your ball and the hole. Can you take out a wedge and chip? Yes. Should you repair that area? Of course.

Walkers And Riders

Pedestrian and motorized golfers can steer clear of conflict

In their ideas about what makes the game superior to other pastimes, experienced golfers usually march side by side down the same road.

Just as it reaches the first tee, however, that road forks, and one half of it turns into a cart path. This is where trouble often starts. Increasingly, golfers who prefer to walk the course are bridling at the omnipresence of motorized carts, to the point that relations among riders and walkers have become stressed and politeness difficult to sustain.

Theoretically, whether a golfer is courteous and well mannered has nothing to do with the issue of walking versus riding. In practice, the potential for on-course conflict is increased by golf carts. It runs highest, of course, when two standard golf-course characters cross paths: the freedom-loving cart

21

rider and the exercise-loving golf purist. The animosity between these two sometimes resembles that of the smoker and the non-smoker.

Even without this study in opposites, golf carts can create problems just by virtue of their bulk, their speed and their capacity for noise and sudden movement. Whether you enjoy riding, dislike it or don't care either way, you have to agree that a round of golf on foot is not the same experience as a round played out of a golf cart.

In fact, when golf carts first became popular in America, they were produced by dozens of different companies and sported much more complicated body designs than those offered by the few manufacturers still in the market. With cheerful model names like the Capri, the Mardi Gras and the Terra-car (so named because it resembled a tortoise), 1960s golf carts reached far beyond function and perhaps helped wedge American golf into the polyester-plaid ghetto it occupied between Vietnam and the Reagan years. On the other hand, as most golfers everywhere know, cart riding has always been uncommon and unpopular in Great Britain.

The reason for sharing this bit of golf-cart history is to point out that riding the course has only been a vital aspect of the golf experience for two generations, and only then in the United States. On that basis, it can't automatically be seen as an eternal facet of the sport. Indeed, if our restrictive rules about the use of paved paths had been common in the 1950s and '60s, walking-and-carrying — not to mention the hiring of caddies — might never have gone out of style. With the recently renewed emphasis on exercise and golf purism, the idea of motorized carts is less widely accepted than it was five or 10 years ago.

However, before leaping to express your own opinion on the subject (especially the anti-riding view that is quickly becoming fashionable) consider a few points:

➤ Some people cannot walk the golf course, be it long or shot, hilly or flat. Age, injury and infirmity were the original reasons for the appearance of golf carts, and they remain valid reasons today.

➤ Some golfers who might enjoy walking haven't thought the matter through and made up their minds to try it. Habit, mandatory-cart rules and their own over-sized baggage has cowed them into seeing cart rental as an essential part of the golf day. They may lack the motivation — in the form of relatives or friends who have suffered from heart disease — that spurs a fellow golfer to embrace walking. Whatever the creed, recent converts are usually shrillest in espousing it. They would do well to remember that part of common courtesy is allowing others some time to come around to one's own enlightened point of view.

➤ There are also golfers who greatly dislike golf carts but are not holier-than-thou about it. Against their preference, they will deign to ride if someone else in the group feels the need to. There are instances when such magnanimity solves a big problem for the foursome.

COMPROMISE: TWO BAGS, ONE RIDER

This brings up a scenario that nowadays is common enough to merit particular attention. What is the proper way to proceed when the number of devoted walkers and riders in a foursome is unequal? Is it acceptable for the devoted walker to say: "I'll put my bag on the cart but I won't ride?" The answer is yes, with certain conditions:

➢ Some sensible arrangement as to the rental fee must be made. Often, the cart-happy golfer will be prepared to pay the entire fee. At high-priced resorts, where cart rental can cost more than a cross-country bus ticket, the payment issue is significant.

➢ The walker cannot give off an attitude of moral superiority. Smugness, never appreciated, is especially inappropriate here, given that the rider will essentially be providing caddie service by ferrying the walker's clubs to his ball, even beginning the search for it when Mr. Walker has missed a fairway.

➢ The cart pilot must not continually ask the walker if he would like a ride. "Aw, c'mon, get in" is an unfair and irritating refrain to have to listen to. The exception would be a long path between holes, especially if it is fully paved, or a severe hill, or both. A retreat from sudden rain might also persuade the traditionalist to break with tradition, although a golf cart is not where you want to be when lightning strikes.

➤ Ironically, though the entire day may go by without the walker riding shotgun even once, there will almost certainly be times when he must drive the cart around to the back or side of the green while Mr. Rider plays a shot from a no-carts area on the opposite side of that green. His alternative is to play his own approach, then walk past the cart, forcing the other party to come all the way back to the buggy in order to bring it forward. That would be inconsiderate, whatever your principles.

➤ In general, the rider will have to be alert to where the walker's ball is. The walker shouldn't have to always wait for the rider to play his own shot, then start wondering where he needs to drive next. In turn, the walker will have to take a handful of clubs with him to his ball at certain times, so the cart can be released and sent forward. This maneuver is required of anyone who allows his clubs to go on a cart, especially now that restricted pathways for carts are so common.

GENERAL ETIQUETTE
FOR CART RIDERS

No matter who you are playing with — inveterate walkers or habitual riders — you must observe a special set of courtesies as you steer around the course in your cart.

In general, the offenses one commits at the wheel of a golf cart victimize the golf course, rather than another golfer. Strategies for preventing wear to the course seem to vary from place to place. Your best bet is to obey the policy set by whatever course you are playing, even when it clashes with your own ideas about how tires harm turfgrass.

Some clubs and courses forbid you to leave the paved cart paths or the rough under any circumstances. Other facilities enforce the so-called 90-degree rule, which requires that you drive along the rough to a point even with your ball (on the fairway) then make a 90-degree turn toward it, retracing that same route back to the rough. Other courses encourage cart drivers to disperse freely over each hole, to keep the rough from receiving undue wear. All courses divert carts away from greens and tees, and virtually all place greater restrictions on cart traffic when the golf course is saturated with rain. A general good citizenship is required of cart users who wish to help spare the playing surface any undue wear.

Make sure you ascertain before you play what the cart rule is for that particular course on that particular day.

In order also to avoid bothering your immediate riding partner or playing partners, you should remember these few points:

➤ The wire basket between the seat and the bag-well is the only safe place for sweaters and other clothing that is donned or shed according to the weather. If you use this basket for clothing and headcovers only, you will never go wrong. Sandwiches, crackers, cookies and other edibles should go in the front dashboard along with balls, gloves and tees. Soiled towels should be hung on the golf bag itself.

➤ Trash tends to accumulate in the dashboard area, too. Some cart riders make it their responsibility to completely fill this area with trash by round's end. It is a considerate gesture to occasionally transfer trash from the cart to one of the 17 wastebaskets you pass along the way.

➤ The phrase "good cart golf" is used humorously when two people riding together both miss the fairway on the same side. Because the two riders generally hit to different spots, there is a constant need to evaluate whose ball should be visited first, and whether the first player brought to his ball should volunteer to walk from there to the spot the cart must next go or whether the one next to play should walk to his ball. Eventually, the time comes when the cart should be parked in the appropriate greenside spot and the players who have not reached the green must take a variety of irons and a putter to wherever their balls lie. Experienced golfers must explain this pattern to novices, or they will ride endlessly around the green chasing their ball.

➤ Especially when you are in a golf cart, but also when you are walking the course, it is thoughtful to remain somewhere along the path between your last green and the next tee until the group on that tee has hit away.

➤ Warning beepers that sound when the cart is shifted into reverse can be highly irritating. Don't activate this beeper until you've checked behind you that there is room to back up.

➤ On cool days, driving a golf cart at its top speed (without a windshield) chills your passenger. If he or she is dressed more lightly than you, restrict your speed. Another time to keep it slow is when you and/or your riding partner have just placed full cups of iced tea or soda in the drink holders.

➤ Whether in the woods or the rough, do not drive in circles looking for a lost ball. Park and search on foot.

➤ Between nines or at the beginning or end of a round, it is possible you will find yourself alone in a cart that is stocked with valuable golf equipment and personal items such as wallets and wristwatches. It is a question of security more than courtesy that you avoid parking the cart and leaving it unguarded in an area where the light-fingered might happen by.

➤ Rule 19-2 provides for loss of hole (in match play) or a two-stroke penalty (in stroke play) if a ball played by oneself or one's partner strikes the golf cart one is riding in. To help your cause, keep that cart out of the way of all shots. The same rule allows one's opponents to replay their shot with no penalty if they hit the cart you're riding in.

It goes without saying that no breach of good manners has any importance whatever compared to an act that puts oneself or others in danger. Every year, golfers are killed and paralyzed due to accidents in golf carts. Safety reminders can be found on bulletin boards at most golf courses as well as printed on the golf cart itself. Ponds, steep terrain, wet grass and congested areas tend to be most hazardous. Three-wheeled carts are much riskier than four-wheeled carts. Think safety on every hole, and don't get in a golf cart with someone who has been drinking. Better yet, rent a pull cart.

C H A P T E R

I V

Courtesy Among Misfits

*Compatability tips when ability
and experience aren't equal*

When Homer Kelley's odd, complex instruction book, *The Golfing Machine*, first appeared in 1969, it was greeted with derision and declared unreadable. Since then, the book has become a cult classic from which most top instructors do a little or a lot of borrowing. In his opening paragraph, Kelley wonders out loud whether golf is a difficult or an easy game, and the first half of his answer is typical of the author's prose — so logical it borders on satire:

*"It is an easy game,
in that no amount of ignorance
about the technique can, alone, prevent
players from completing the trip from
Tee to Cup."*

In this wry way, Kelley echoes the favorite observation of golf's boosters; namely, that players of all levels can go out on the course together and share the game's pleasures regardless of their relative abilities. What's more, they can even compete head-to-head, using the miracle of the handicap system to offset their inherent skill disparity.

On one side of the coin we have this sanguine observation about the game's basic structure. Turn the coin around, and we see before our eyes the countless, untold descents into shame and mortification experienced by unskilled golfers in the presence of skilled golfers. To skull, whiff, shank, duck-hook and push-slice your way around the course, then turn to three people who have all shot rounds in the 80s and say, "Great game, golf — all skill levels can play together in harmony," denies the reality of human feelings.

Regardless of the effort we make to refine our on-course social graces, we will find them tested strenuously by situations that throw the incompetent in with the competent. It shouldn't have to be this way. Golf is not like ballroom dancing, where one participant's clumsiness prevents his partner from performing skillfully. If anything, a shaky golfer makes those around him look good by comparison. Yet, the times when oafish play most disgraces the oaf are the times when he feels he has singlehandedly destroyed one of God's afternoons, no matter how sunny the weather, no matter how well the other golfers played.

This entire nightmare, by the way, is not the province of the raw beginner. At the very start of every golf career there is some degree of refuge from judgment, either by outsiders or oneself. But in Year Two or

Three, and ever after, the embarrassment apparatus is fully in place. Scoring at the triple- and quadruple-bogey level and beyond, any non-rookie golfer is likely to fear that, vis-a-vis the better players around him, he will slow up play, affect the form and tempo of others, chew up the golf course, force continual searching for his ball, etc. He must instead accept this basic truth: You don't have to be a good golfer to be a good person to play golf with.

MAINTAINING LEVITY REQUIRES A GROUP EFFORT

Handicap system or no handicap system, you'll notice that a huge collective effort is made by the golfing public to huddle into foursomes of relatively equal skill level. Still, there are many exceptions to this pattern, such as when one member of a vacationing couple ventures onto the resort golf course as a single, or when a bachelor party or college reunion committee coerces semi-golfers into signing up for the golf outing. Because golf has evolved into an almost compulsory business skill, (somewhere on the core curriculum between speech giving and spreadsheet reading) the opportunities for embarrassment of poor players has increased all the more.

But, as Eleanor Roosevelt said, no one can make you feel inferior without your consent. Applying this principle to the 18-hole fiasco in which Tom, Dick and Harry play decent golf, but Walter plays jaw-droppingly awful golf, we come up with some suggestions for each party to consider.

PROTOCOL FOR THE INEPT ONE

➢ Smile At Anything In Play. Etiquette requires that a golfer help his companions search for lost balls. Searching for your ball is something those playing with you will soon tire of. Therefore, your low, scuttling straight shot that travels safely to the start of the fairway will be a relief to them. Let it be a relief to you as well. No matter whether you are breaking par or not breaking 100, declining help in the search for lost balls is the responsibility of all golfers. You can permit others to help for a minute or two, but let them off the hook after that — especially if you no longer care about your score for that hole, and are only continuing to hunt because you don't want to lose two dollars worth of sporting goods.

➢ Pick Up, Judiciously. In the British Isles, where golf was invented, picking up your ball is normal procedure once you've fouled up a hole. Someone playing miserably should pick up about four or five times in 18 holes. More than six and you might as well not be out there. Often, you will "pick up" in name only, as once again your ball is lost or drowned. Don't mope, just do it. Remind yourself that good players pick up probably more often than lousy players, in this country, anyway. Remember that absolute maximum score is double the par for that hole. Once you get to the "snowman" level of 8 on a par-4 hole, for example, you owe no further effort to the cause.

➤ Don't Start Analyzing Your Swing. It's not unthinkable that your wild misses and comical gouging could be largely cured by a quick tip from someone in the group. If one is offered, give it a try. But if it doesn't work, don't keep turning to the amateurs around you for further Band-Aids. And refrain from gasping out diagnoses as each swing ends and the ball begins its pitiful trickle. It's a simple problem; you need only two things: lessons and practice.

➤ Carry Off All Non-Golf Acts Without Incident. On this day, you can't do anything right with a club and ball. But you can remove and replace headcovers without misplacing them. You can, with concentration, slip quarters into a soda machine and apply mustard to a hot dog. Let the breaks from golf be breaks from your ineptitude. When someone makes a 12 on a hole — that's just golf. When he follows it up by dumping coffee on his lap, you start believing you've got a wall-to-wall spaz on your hands.

➤ Don't Save Face by Alluding to Other Achievements. You may be rich, you may hang out with celebrities, you may have invented gel shave cream. None of that will help you now. Chumps who hit wild slices toward the parking lot and use this as an excuse to mention "my Porsche" are the people who supply groups of golf buddies with the classic running gags they replay forever.

➤ The Obvious Stuff. Track your ball relentlessly; looking away in disgust only means more search work for others. Hit a provisional ball every once in a while. Pay some attention to the other players: don't be the only one who doesn't realize that Harry's putting for a 3 on a par-5. Don't moan. Don't blame your equipment. Tend your share of pins. Try to learn one little thing that will help your game in the future.

➤ Don't Praise Others' Shots Simply Because They Get Airborne. A golfer who can't do anything right tends to say "Good shot" whenever someone he's playing with makes solid contact. Then, when the ball flies over the green into a swamp, the player who hit it has insult added to his injury. Try to see fellow players' shots through their eyes.

PROCEDURES FOR THOSE AROUND HIM

➤ Ignore Him, Distract Him. The klutz you are paired with may have heard the very-true truism that golfers notice other golfers' games much less than the others imagine. Act as living proof of this statement. Slip into a Mr. Magoo mode: you see him, you just don't see his shots. When possible, talk about movies, pro sports, states where the price of gasoline is unusually high or low.

➤ Yell "Fore" On His Behalf. Along about the fifth time we hit a shot that threatens the safety of others, frustration and shame tend to shut down our vocal cords. Silence in golf can be fatal. When playing with someone who is having an awful day, be ever alert to shout warnings.

➢ When You Have a Bad Hole Yourself, Shrug It Off. If perfectionism is your basic mode, the Golf Gods may be telling you to abandon it today. Someone who can't do a thing right may not be able to stand seeing you fume over the only three-putt of the day.

➢ Talk to Him about Something He's Good At. It's no good if he brings it up, but if you're the one to get a conversation going about a field he's successful in, you might be able to remove some of the pall from the afternoon. You may even get a job offer out of it.

➢ Feel Free Not to Comment on His Shots. Attempts to find something good in a long series of misguided shots eventually become absurd. Skip the faint praise, however well meant.

Anyone can enjoy golf when the whole group is playing well and the birds are twittering, etc. It's only as great a game as we all say it is if some enjoyment and reward can be had on a day when players appear to be doing all they can to humiliate themselves. If you're the accursed one, try to show some grace under pressure. If you aren't, try to help the patient stagger home with a few shreds of self-esteem. There are many stories of accomplished players whose games have completely deserted them for years, sometimes forever. Maybe it all started on a day when they showed no sympathy for a golf soul adrift.

C H A P T E R

V

The Role Of The Guest

*A host of ways to make sure your
first invitation isn't your last*

One summer in the late 1970s, at a prominent country club outside Boston, a player on the local professional basketball team became a frequent guest. Though not an experienced golfer, he was, of course, a natural athlete and improved rapidly. One Saturday morning, playing as Mr. Smith's guest, he shot an 87 and told good stories in the grill room. The next Saturday, playing as Mr. Jones's guest, he managed an 82 and followed with more storytelling. So it went, until the basketball player began arriving every Saturday morning at no particular invitation, but rather as a guest-at-large for the club in general to absorb. Finally, of course, a club officer invited him to not come round at all.

Golf is just one among hundreds of settings in which we enact the ancient ritual of inviting and accepting, hosting and guesting. From an afternoon sail to an all-night poker game, every venue that mixes the owner or the regular

patrons with an invited guest has guidelines
— spoken or unspoken — that are intended
to insure harmonious interaction and a good
time for all.

Among the guidelines suggested here, one
very familiar host-and-guest pattern in golf
will receive only slight mention. The pattern
in question involves two golfers who belong
to different clubs and each hosts the other at
his or her annual member-guest tournament.
If two men or two women who team up twice
a year to compete and socialize at each
other's clubs still need advice as to their conduct in these settings, it must be that they
have already been given such advice and
either not heard it or not heeded it.

As for that basketball star who overstayed
his welcome, the somewhat ironic point of
the story is this: When you are invited to a
golf club by one of its members, you actually
become the guest of the entire membership.
There is a collective responsibility on their
part to make you feel welcome, and a
requirement on your part that your presence
will grace, not terrorize, their little enclave.

Taking this point to the extreme case, you
need to bear in mind that a day spent as a
guest is, for 90 percent of all nonrelatives who
eventually join a private club, the first step
toward eventual membership. Even
if belonging to Stately Oaks C.C. is the furthest thing from your mind when you accept
an invitation to play there, some members
may be looking at you as someone who
intends to join. When you come to understand the inflated degree of pride many
people take in their country clubs, you'll real-

ize how natural it is for them to assume that simply everyone wants to belong there.

THE GUEST'S GUIDE:
ROBERT'S RULES TO MURPHY'S LAW

When a golfer who belongs to a private club is introduced to a golfer who does not, a silly thing often happens. If their acquaintance is marked by instant warmth (or if one of the two golfers is marrying into the other's family), the club member will almost automatically mention that it would be nice to have the other party over to his club for a round of golf. If the other party responds by whipping out an appointment book and discussing dates, the face of the club member will likely freeze in place. He didn't really mean it.

These pre-invitations, however noncommittal, are not borne of insincerity. In most cases, the dues-payer has virtually no choice. The fact is, golfers cannot spend any time in each other's presence without turning the conversation to its rightful topic. Once the forum is opened, it's only a matter of moments before the question, "Where do you play?" is uttered. "I'm a member at _____" then goes on the record, and whoever says it can only hope the other is a member somewhere, as well. If the other person is unattached, the club member, on behalf of all right-minded club members the world over, will feel obliged to at least mention that "it would be nice."

Your first duty as a golf guest, therefore, is to accept the non-invitation in the spirit in which it was made, and shrug off the fact that no formal offer follows. If you are a public links golfer and your comings and goings put you in frequent contact with club golfers, you may even develop conversational tricks that allow for golf to be discussed in earnest but steer you clear of those moments when vague invitations would seem called for.

Once the honor of your presence is requested and a golf date is made official, you will want to try to guarantee yourself a smooth path from your doorstep to the first tee. Face it, showing good form is half the challenge in any social engagement; in golf the ratio is probably more like three-quarters. If your sense of style prevents you from reducing your golf rendezvous to the following NASA-countdown specifics, then maybe you've got the élan it takes to survive a late, harried arrival and the wrong clothing. If you don't, check off the following:

➤ When You're Expected. The key coordinate is usually your tee time, but that's just the beginning. If the pro shop has you and your esteemed host down for 9:48, your natural arrival time at the parking lot would be between 8:30 and 9:00. This provides time for socializing, hitting practice balls on the driving range, warming up your putter on the putting green, changing clothes and/or shoes and sitting down for coffee. If you are to play a morning round, the likely meal you will be offered is lunch after you play, not breakfast before. So, you're unlikely to go wrong by having toast and cereal at home before heading off. If the course you are playing has no set tee times, you may want to press your host for specifics on when you should arrive and when your group is likely to go off.

➤ Arrival. Even before you leave your house, make sure to find out the dress code for the course to be played. Most courses require a collared shirt and shorts of a certain length, but some don't allow shorts at all.

If you have seldom or never been to this particular golf course, get to-the-letter directions and write them legibly. If the directions your host gives you seem at all shaky, call the golf shop. Don't get directions that stop at the entrance gate; given the manorial scattering of the buildings on some older club properties, you have to be super-alert not to and just end up at the maintenance shed or detoured off the property onto some confusing boulevard. Determine your exact path through the facility.

You may be expected to pull up to a "Bag Drop" and pop open your trunk for an attendant who then removes your clubs. If there is no bag drop, then your challenge is to carry your clubs directly to the spot where they will stay while you change your shoes, drink coffee, get shown the historic trophies, etc. You don't want to be walking all around the property with your equipment, nor do you want to have left it in some odd spot when everyone else's gear is assembled where the staff can organize it onto golf carts or caddies' shoulders. At many clubs, the locker room attendants will know that you are expected and will be able to tell you where your host can be found and where you may dress and/or store personal items.

Your golf shoes can cause minor awkwardness in several ways:

➤ You can put them on publinx-style back in the parking lot, and then end up barred from the clubhouse tour your host is so fond of conducting (no spikes in the dining room, etc.).

➤ You can leave them zipped in your golf bag and have the golf bag whisked to a place where you certainly don't want to be seen changing shoes.

➤ You can carry them with you loose or in some unsightly plastic bag.

Moral of the story: Get a proper drawstring shoe bag and carry your spikes in it until you are shown to a bench in the locker room where you will change. One final note on shoes: If you're wearing footwear that can be polished or spiffed up in any way, the locker room shoe attendants will spiff them up for you, and you will tip them from $2 to $5.

THE PRELIMINARIES

Inexperienced golfers are no different from veterans in how they hope a day like this will turn out. Basically, we all carry two objectives: to appear at ease and to play well. The ideal situation is to arrive on time or a little early, proceed leisurely to a meeting spot with your host, relax over coffee and talk about the golf course and the weather, then get in 20 to 30 minutes of productive warmups on the range and the putting green.

If you are feeling capable of horrid golf that day (haven't played in weeks, played poorly last time, etc.), you may find yourself obsessed with getting to the range and hitting five buckets of balls. Don't fall into this trap. Often the warm-up opportunity will be frittered away by the host showing you around or buying something in the shop or clearing up some confusion with the golf professionals. Your mulligan may be your only practice shot. If that's how things turn out, just make your peace with it.

➤ Betting and Matches. Whatever the host suggests is probably what you'll do. If you don't have an official handicap from the course you play, let your host know in advance; he and the others will try to figure out a ballpark handicap for you and use that in figuring the bets.

One way to offset the lack of official handicaps is to play a game called Honest John. It's actually an overlay bet of a couple of dollars, with the winner being the person whose final gross score is closest to what he predicted he would shoot. Theoretically, it prevents someone from sandbagging the group by saying he has a handicap that's actually higher than what he deserves. If you say you are a 15-handicap, you'll be expected to shoot about 88-90. If you make the typical sandbagger move of saying you're a 15 and then shoot an 82, you'll lose your chance at the Honest John pot. Obviously, the two bets have to be somewhat in line with each other. The other bet, by the way, will probably be a nassau or a skins game. Nassau divides the round into three parts (front side, back side, total 18) while skins takes each hole as a separate bet with a winner (or a carryover) on every green.

➤ Money Matters. Whether you plan to win or lose whatever bets are made, it's a good idea to arm yourself with a supply of small bills. You'll probably tip the shoe-room attendant, the person who loads your clubs on and off golf carts and washes them when the round is over, and perhaps a beverage cart operator or someone manning a refreshment stand out on the golf course.

At a private club, it's possible that the only significant expenditures you may make are to pay caddies their fees and tips. If your host permits it, this may be more than a nice gesture. Caddie fees at major golf clubs around the big cities can run from $25 to $50 per bag for 18 holes. Cart fees, which the member will sign for, are usually less than the caddie fees. If you decide to take care of the caddie fees, do so as you come up the 18th hole, or risk being overruled later.

Because virtually all outlays have to be signed for by a member, hosts don't usually have to make a big deal about the guest not reaching into his or her pocket. In the golf shop, your cash will almost certainly be welcomed. It is ceremonial, in some quarters, for the host to buy a dozen balls and hand out sleeves to his guest or guests. That doesn't prevent you from buying a dozen yourself and offering them around. If you decide you want to purchase a cap, visor, sweater or shirt, you should probably tell your host of your intentions, lest he worry you'll spend a half-hour shopping and trying things on. In all likelihood, you'll get some points for having patronized the golf shop. Think twice about buying a shirt crested with the club name, however; you may grow to feel conspicuous wearing it after several people ask you whether you are, indeed, a member of this club.

At a facility where cash is accepted, a semi-private or public course, these restraints are not as clear cut. Your host will either have to be more explicit in his instructions about what you may offer to pay for, or you will have to fill in the gaps instinctively. Recently, the no-cash policies of some clubs seem to have been relaxed, allowing for the use of legal tender at halfway houses, at least.

There are in fact times when offering to pay entry fees and other costs associated with team tournaments is quite appropriate. Among golfers who are active in their local tournament circuit, it's common to extend an invitation on the basis of needing a partner rather than wishing to play the magnanimous host.

➢ In General. The actual round of golf may not be much different than if you had met at a neutral site. The member will of course offer advice and information about the course and how to play it, but that could happen anywhere two golfers play if one knows the course and the other doesn't. Some club members turn this course-guide into an extension of the morning's clubhouse tour, dispensing facts and stories that overload the non-member with club trivia. While irritating, this kind of patter comes under the heading of the-price-you-pay for a day of golf.

➢ Returning the Favor. In cases where members of different clubs invite each other to play as guests at their respective facilities, reciprocating is a fairly simple matter. The one tricky spot would involve a club's three-or-four-day member-guest, the big annual event complete with stag parties and dinner dances. Inviting a guest to one of these events is a major investment in a relationship, be it social, business or family. If you are the recipient of such an invitation, and you are already committed to hosting someone else at your own club's big member-guest, you may want to decline politely. If you can look forward to a time when you can have this person as your guest at a major function, you may feel freer to accept.

If you have no club to which you can take someone who has generously hosted you, the best option may be to reciprocate by sending along a gift or having your benefactor to dinner.

It Isn't Hard To Be A Good Guest

Many factors will affect your host's attitude toward offers of reimbursement for guest fees. His company's prosperity, your status as a customer or prospect, the latest IRS statement on business-entertainment deductions, whether or not the monthly dining-room minimum has been reached, etc. In some cases there will be no doubt that your money is unwanted, but not always. Ironically, the more your relationship with the host veers toward friendship and away from pure business, the more appropriate it would be for you to ante up.

It is best to settle these questions well in advance of the moment of truth, which arrives when you sign the guest book in the golf shop and all guest fees are payable. Unlike a waiter's delivery of your dinner check to the restaurant table, golf fee payments come due with all manner of strangers and fellow club members elbowing at the same counter. There have been cases in which a host who had rehearsed a spontaneous, lighthearted, "Well, if you insist," was struck dumb by the sudden appearance of fellow members who would witness his lack of largesse. In general, a thoughtful guest will be capable of smooth, unobtrusive profferings that a host can accept without losing face.

It sounds simplistic, but all most people want is for their guests to relax and enjoy themselves. Often, there is no better way of showing one's appreciation than to smile and spread cheer. In golf, if you are playing poorly, the critical factor is to keep trying to play well without lapsing into constant complaint or self-flagellation. If you do happen to embarrass yourself, find a golf professional with a keen eye and get down to the tough business of improving your game.

With All Deliberate Speed

*The thoughtful golfer's internal clock
and how it ticks*

At a club where I caddied as a boy, two surgeons would emerge from the men's grill every Wednesday at a little past noon and head toward the first tee. Moments earlier, the caddiemaster would have appeared before his T-shirted work force to utter five words: Your own last name (you dearly hoped), then, "Dr. McKenna, Dr. Klein."

A shiver of profound gratitude would run down your shoulders, then two heavy bags would descend on them to create an opposite sensation. From that moment on, barring a course-closing typhoon, it would be no fewer than seven hours and just about 160 strokes for each player before the day ended. All the same, that was a coveted twosome. Figured it out yet? The good doctors went around twice.

There are legions of slow-paced golfers who want only what these two men wanted — to spend the day on the golf course. But, unlike the two doctors, who were rewarded for their swiftness by being able to play 36 holes, many public golfers would gain little by going around in 3:15. Basically, they would be off the golf course — which they had waited all week to get on — after what seemed like a very brief period of time.

On the rare occasions when we complete 18 holes in three hours and a few minutes, most of us sense that our appetites for golf are not sated. We feel the urge to head right back out. Even if we all agree that faster play often means better play, isn't there good evidence that barrelling along briskly is not, deep down, what most people want to do?

Which brings us to the ironic, problematic truth about golf etiquette and speed of play: When Player A commits a delay-causing act, Player B (or C or D) may have to call him on it. Because the foursome as a unit is responsible for holdups, the laggard will often have to be confronted with his or her wrongdoing. This is not true of other breaches. Someone who talks during other players' backswings could be endured for 18 holes and then avoided ever after. Someone who doesn't replace his divots could be followed around and cleaned up after, until he got the point. Someone who thoughtlessly says, "Good one" about an important shot of yours that is drifting out of bounds can be handled by a roll of the eyes and a silent curse. But the dawdler, who sins against society at large, cannot be tolerated stoically.

In the endless battle to counteract televised golf's example of slow-pro golf, here are some tips and hints to help you herd the dilly-dallyers along:

➤ Get Off to a Good Start: On the first tee, having a ball teed and its owner ready to hit as soon as the way is clear should be easy; on the other hand, arranging bets and making acquaintances are powerful distractions. Conclude these preparations as quickly as possible. Also, count your own clubs and ask whether anyone left putters or wedges by the practice green. Always assume the group that just hit off will vacate the first fairway quickly. If you're having trouble choosing teams and setting up wagers, take a ball from each player, throw all four in the air and have the two closest be a team. Ask that a long story be saved for later. Always note the exact time (it is seldom the scheduled time) the first ball was struck, and announce it to the group.

➤ Play in Groups No Larger Than Four: In general, fivesomes are a breach of course or club rules.

➤ Get Familiar with the Course Map and Markings: There's not much excuse for taking six or seven holes to realize that the dwarf spruce trees mark 150 yards and that a white brick signifies 100. Look ahead on the card to determine the next par-3 hole's yardage. This will help avoid having players walk up a hill to the tee, look around, then walk back down to the bag for a club. Also, whenever you pass the green of a hole you will play later, note the pin position and any unseen trouble. An hour later, when your group is looking up at this green from a valley, you will be able to say, "Pin is 15 yards from the front; if you overshoot it you'll just be in some light rough."

➤ Early Holdups Are Often Overcome: There is no excuse for falling into a group attitude of hopelessness just because you waited five minutes on the third tee. "We were getting held up every other hole on the front side" is a lame lament for a foursome that, wonder of wonders, has two holes open ahead of it on the back nine. Even if true, it is irrelevant to the present situation; what is revealed is that they gave up trying to play at a proper pace. As long as there are golfers behind you, you can't give up the fight.

➤ When You Have to Leave Wedges at Greenside: Get in the habit of leaving them next to clubs that other members of the group have set aside, or on top of the pulled pin. It's almost impossible that three people would forget to pick up their clubs, and quite unlikely that no one would remember to replace the flagstick. Another good idea is to leave these clubs on a spot you have to walk past to get to the next hole.

➤ Keep Extra Balls in Your Pocket: If you have to hit a provisional ball or take a drop, it's quicker to reach into your pocket than to walk to your bag.

➤ Attend to the Slow Player: Often one player is the reason that four are making poor time. Identify the member of your group who is at fault and do what you can to help. Mark his ball's direction and help him head straight toward it. Talk about the next hole and ask him what club he plans to use. Eventually you'll have to be more blunt, but you can start with the nice-guy approach.

➢ Limit the Exchange of Advice: If you can read your fourball partner's putt while he's waiting to play, read all you like. Just remember that team strategizing is a major cause of slow play.

➢ If You're Falling Behind, Take Gradual Measures: Some people swear by a system called "Ready Golf." Among other measures, this system does away with the proud traditions of honor on the tee and he-furthest-from-the-hole-plays-next. With Ready Golf, any player who is prepared to hit may do so. If you prefer to observe the strict protocol of playing in turn, perhaps your foursome could agree to invoke the Ready concept only when it is lagging far behind, and then revert to form when it has caught up to the group ahead.

➢ Invoke the Leaf Rule: Fall is a lovely time for golf, but searching through the leaves for a ball is inefficient and usually futile. Agree on a no-penalty "leaf rule" at the beginning of your autumn rounds, and live by it. This rule permits a player to drop a ball at a point as close as possible to where his ball presumably entered the leaves.

➢ Heed the Hazard Markings and Read the Scorecard: Much time is wasted by people who play provisional tee shots when the area they have hit into is a lateral hazard (marked with red stakes) that allows relief at the point where the ball entered the area. To re-tee in such an instance serves no purpose, except perhaps to raise your eventual score.

➤ Play from the Appropriate Tees: If your whole group can break 80, maybe the back tees are what you want. Most people should avoid them, increasing their pleasure in the process. If two aces are paired with a high-handicapper, the high-handicapper should play from a different spot than the aces choose. Etiquette demands that you play from a set of markers, rather than from improvised points such as the ball washers. If your course's markers don't suit your game, tell the people in charge.

SPEEDING UP SOMETIMES CALLS FOR SACRIFICES

You're out of the hole, but the putt you have is a downhill breaker that you're especially good at. Or, you brought your pitching wedge and 9-iron from the cart, and now realize your long, uphill chip really requires an 8-iron. All golfers pontificate about how awful slow play is, but how many are willing to sacrifice some private enjoyment or even a stroke on the scorecard in the name of quickness?

Foursomes who are causing delays should be willing to give each other putts they normally would prefer to see made. They should even forego a hot dog and a soda at the turn (for some this would be the supreme sacrifice) to make up lost time.

The classic sacrifice is to step aside and let the group behind play through. This is a sensitive moment, particularly if the tailgaters have actually requested they be let through.

Some, by the way, consider asking as always inappropriate; others feel it rights two wrongs and therefore must be allowable. At a public course, give a slow group ahead two holes to either speed up or allow you through. If this approach fails, feel free to politely ask to play through or have a ranger ask them to yield. At a private club, don't ask to be let through; chronically slow golfers will be spoken to by the golf committee.

When the British writer Bernard Darwin said, "No one ever played a good hole when playing through," he pointed up the difficulty of taking over a hole from other golfers and still resisting the urge to rush. In cases where a twosome or single is passing a threesome or foursome, the problem really should not occur, although it is always the responsibility of a yielding group to convince the passers, via words and gestures, to play at a normal, relaxed pace. As a member of the yielding group, you may be best off devoting a few minutes to the organizational or cleanup projects one usually has no time for, such as folding sweaters, discarding trash, filling in missed scores on the card, etc.

Of course, long before the idea of playing through is broached, a foursome has told the one in back of it a lot about itself. Little things — always having the pin poised while the last player putts, and being willing to walk off the wrong side of the green, relative to where your next hole is, so that their play can restart more quickly — these things convey a message of thoughtfulness that will help avoid resentment later.

In the chapters on guests and hosts, we will see that the pace of play can be a ticklish point between an invited guest and his patron. The only way to avoid difficulty is for the guest to play along at a nice clip without having to pick up his ball regularly, which most hosts would find unsatisfactory.

The need to keep planning shots and moving forward is why golfers set aside the 19th Hole for detailed analysis of the day's play. There is time for some storytelling and chitchat as you play, but there's much less of it than a beginning golfer would guess. When four experienced players go out for 18 holes with only three hours of daylight left, their efficiency will rival that of a yacht crew on race day. Checking distances, selecting clubs, replacing divots, reading greens, marking scores: all these little acts will be happening quickly, constantly and automatically.

In the end, holdups result from a group's ingrained, overall slowness or from exceptional cases of delay. Among the latter, a lost ball is by far the most common. The rule book allows five minutes maximum, but some ignore the rule altogether and some suspend it for balls that are crucial to a match. Obviously, playing a provisional ball from the spot where the suspected lost ball was launched is the only way to proceed under the rules without walking back to that original spot.

When a ball must be searched for, the player who hit it is responsible for shooing away help from members of the foursome who have their own search to conduct, or whose balls are on the opposite side of the fairway, or who have difficult shots (bunkered, blind, etc.) to prepare for. Extended searches for balls that have no significance to a match or to a medal score are the worst offenses, particularly when conducted by people of some means who economize nowhere else other than with golf balls. At one course in Wisconsin, rangers immediately hand a new ball, free of charge, to any searchers who threaten to hold up play. To some slow-play fighters, the mere presence of a ball retriever in your bag is a breach of courtesy.

Slow play is indeed the one context in which accusation making is sanctioned, but it is also the place where you can overstep your rights — or be downright wrong — when you speak up. Perhaps the greatest potential for dispute lies in the difference of opinion as to something like practice swings. Without going into complexities, some golfers would say that making good shots speeds you up, and making inaccurate shots slows you down. On that basis, whatever it takes to play down the middle is probably worth it. Others say, avoid delays of any kind and you'll always keep pace. Practice swings tend to be the focus of this debate, and the advice here is to make an honest evaluation and proceed accordingly. If a player is aware of the clock and of those around him, that's at least half the battle. Play well, and play at a good pace.

C H A P T E R

V I I

Golf's Sacred and Profane Customs

*Why do we tolerate the official rules
but revere the local ones?*

When three or more male golfers are gathered on a reasonably remote tee, and one of them dribbles his drive so weakly that the ball fails to reach the women's tee markers, an obscure provision known as the Texas Rule (a.k.a. the Ft. Worth Rule) presumably goes into effect.

Reflecting the comic brilliance of the collective male mind, the Texas Rule requires the player who struck the miserable drive to immediately modify the manner in which he wears his trousers. This accomplished, he walks to where his ball came to rest, resumes his original, lawful mode of dress and plays his second shot. As reasonable people might expect, this custom — golf's only vulgar one? — is far more honored in the breach than in the observance. It is included in this book so that the innocent may be given notice to prepare a deflectingly witty rejoinder, should they ever fall under the rule's jurisdiction. Quite possibly, this vestigial bit of bawdiness will fail the test of time. However, it does have going for it its effectiveness as comic relief for a situation that some would find more embarrassing than the sentence contained in the rule.

Within situations not covered by the official rules of the game and the general rules of human courtesy, golf presents a busy docket of questions that probe group attitudes and demand a collective decision, consensus or otherwise. Should we play for something? What tees do we play from? Preferred lies or no? Give all putts inside the leather? Attention should be paid to the manner in which these questions are resolved.

Most of a foursome's choices address the question: How relatively difficult, or easy, are we going to make this game? Historically, skill level has not been the characteristic that has determined whether the path of least or greatest resistance will be followed. There are hackers who eschew mulligans and always play the ball as it lies, and there are ace golfers who avail themselves of every waiver and forbearance under the sun.

The more competitive your party, the more important it is to anticipate all the debatable situations and agree beforehand how to treat them. The way to take the fun out of any challenge is to make up the rules as you go along. Where a bet is involved, mid-stream amendments create not only confusion and discontinuity, but resentment and a feeling of having been

cheated, as well. In club golf, and sometimes at public courses, certain of the basic
procedural decisions are made for us. The
obvious ground rule set by committee
involves preferred lies. When the fairways
are in top condition, the chalkboard in the
locker room will read: "Play ball down" or
"Summer rules." When the closely-mown
areas of the course are not uniformly
conditioned, that board should read:
"Play ball up" or "Winter rules" (preferred
lies in fairway).

Another oft-posted ground rule or local
rule addresses the unusual difficulty of finding balls that land amid fallen autumn
leaves. "Leaf rule in effect" is what the club
chalkboard might say to notify players that
Rule 27's stroke-and-distance penalty for a
lost ball is waived. This is an equitable rul-
ing, as long as the lost ball would be find-
able during any other time of the year.
Some committee people who decide these
matters go so far as to identify the holes on
which, after inspection, they feel a leaf provision truly applies.

Once a preferred-lie or leaf rule is posted, the field quickly divides itself into two
constituencies, the abusers and the fair
players. The abusers, on days when the ball
is played up, do not merely reposition their
ball, they enthrone it. Rather than seek
relief from an unfairly harsh fairway lie by
rolling the ball a few inches over or back,
they make sure to exploit every favorable
aspect of stance, sightline and turf surface
within a five-foot radius.

These are the same wretches who adore the fall foliage season not for its glorious colors, but for the expectation that it will exempt them from all further stroke-and-distance penalties on lost balls. Any shot that even glimmers with the possibility of being unfindable sends them marching straight to the nearest leafy area, where they take a free drop and play on, even though their original ball is likely to have disappeared into a hayfield 20 yards to the right. Fair players take warning: you have no recourse but to track the abuser's errant shot all the way to its exact landing point in the hayfield and pull it from the straw as damning evidence.

If you are a guest at a club or playing your first round at a public course with one of its regular denizens, you are obliged to observe, in relative silence, the local rules followed there. Usually you can find them posted in full on a bulletin board near the first tee. If one or more of them clash with your own philosophy of how golf should be played, you should probably voice your dissenting view in an offhand kind of tone.

Problems of interpretation can arise from committee-imposed local rules, and they can also arise from policies put in place by the foursome itself. But most disagreements can be averted through a quick, comprehensive discussion prior to tee-off. The traditional meeting at home plate before a baseball game, in which lineup cards are exchanged and ground rules reviewed, should be adopted in some form by golfers who would have any reason to later regret not doing so. Among the issues to address:

➤ Are mulligans an option on the first tee? Some golfers even favor a "hit till you're happy" policy, although most course owners or starters will be quite unhappy to see the first tee turned into a practice range. If the mulligan is opted for, must it be used, or can the player decide to play his first attempt? Some even differentiate by using the term "finnegan" to describe a free second tee shot that the player is not obliged to use. Finally, if a player's first drive is satisfactory to him, may he save up his mulligan and "travel" with it?

➤ Are putts of a certain length automatically good? Whether or not an "inside the leather" policy is formally adopted, you should know by now that conceding putts is a part of golf's tradition that requires a modicum of judgment, tact and compassion. If you are the kind of golfer who uses putt-conceding as a weapon in your gamesmanship arsenal, no primer such as this can influence your tactics. If you aren't, you should be able to look back at your recent rounds and conclude that you chose appropriate moments to say, "Good by me" or "Pick that one up."

➤ If preferred lies aren't dictated by the golf committee or course ownership, are they to be allowed in this particular group?

➤ If fallen leaves — or excessively high rough that hasn't been cut because the turf is too wet — threatens to make decent shots unfindable, will the group waive stroke-and-distance penalties and allow a free drop?

➢ What brand and number of ball is everyone playing? Remember: to play a ball that you are not able to identify can create major annoyances and holdups. Especially when people are traipsing through leg-scraping thickets out of the goodness of their hearts, you must be able to tell them what they're looking for. Further, if a situation arises in which two balls of the same brand and number land next to one another and cannot be told apart, each ball would be declared lost and the players would have to return to the tee. In an informal game, this penalty would be waived, but your thoughtlessness would be noticed.

➢ The one-ball rule, which prohibits a player from playing tee to green with a "distance ball" then taking out a tour-style ball (presumably more true-putting by its construction) when on the green, doesn't get much attention these days. That doesn't mean you wouldn't be called on it by your fellow competitors if you began breaching it regularly. In fact, the rule is not part of the Rules of Golf, but its use by the PGA Tour is officially approved by the game's rules makers.

Betting is extremely prevalent in golf. In fact, it's considerably more common than paying off is. Some golfers can't stand the fact that others will cheerily agree to a nassau on the first tee and then decline to pay off or to accept a payoff when the round is over. Other golfers consider this a harmless lapse. Apparently, the pretense of risk is enough to "make it interesting" for them, whereas exchanging dollar bills afterward seems superfluous.

The solution is to pay off on any lost bets or not play for money at all. Those who enjoy wagering and revel in all its variations should bear in mind that some golfers like a simple nassau (a three-way bet on the front nine, back nine and full 18) but dislike all the pressing and renegotiating and refiguring that complicated wagers entail. A non-bettor who loses big in a round of business golf should consider reporting the loss as a business expense. It wouldn't be the first time.

Golf With a Caddie

How a proper guide can make your golfing trails happier

"Farrell's Caddie" is John Updike's haunting, amusing short story about a Scottish caddie who is able to see clear into the soul of the agitated American tourist whose clubs he totes for several days. For all its surrealism, the story stands on a solid premise; namely, that golf with an intuitive, assertive caddie can be an educational experience — one in which a person's golfing character comes up for intense scrutiny and eventual judgment.

At the other end of the spectrum from the omniscient caddies of Scotland (and, to a lesser degree, California's Monterrey Peninsula) are the laconic 14-year-olds who do weekend duty at America's suburban country clubs. There is not much clan resemblance between storied Scotsmen like Old Fiery and the "Caddyshack" types whose loop money buys skateboards and stereo systems. But, taken together, these old and young, breezy and gruff, casual and dedicated workers comprise one of golf's most venerable institutions. To know the game in all its fullness, a golfer must not ignore this aspect. Caddying may be uncontracted manual labor, but its glories — including well-endowed scholarship funds and six-figure salaries for its top practitioners — elevate it above most other blue-collar jobs.

Golfers who possess no knowledge of the role in golf history played by Eddie Lowery, Herman Mitchell, Angelo Argea, Bruce Edwards, Golfball and others, may want to expand their horizons beyond the dashboard of their gas-powered E-Z-Go's. Those who actually go so far as to hire their first caddie, however, may need to prepare themselves mentally for the vitality and imperfections of a human club conveyer. Unlike their mechanized replacements, caddies are a diverse lot. Here's how a well-traveled golfer deals with them:

➤ Determine exactly what the fee will be, who in the group is expected to pay what, and what services will be rendered. At a resort or a large country club, the sale of a caddie's services can be a complex transaction. The golfers whose clubs are actually carried receive the labor of the toting, plus bunker raking, divot replacement, pin tending, strategic advice and sometimes encouragement. In return, each pays a fee of between $15 and $40. On top of the fee, they are expected to pay a tip of 20 to 30 percent.

Other members of the foursome who do not hire their own caddie also receive advice and secondary services such as forecaddying, bunker raking, etc. Typically, they are asked to pay a combined fee-tip that equals about one-fourth of what the primary clients pay. In many cases, they will only be expected to produce a tip, say $5 or $10. At some facilities, the hiring of a forecaddie to walk ahead of a foursome's two carts and perform all non-carrying functions of a caddie is a requirement.

However, where it is strictly an option, the players who opt to have their bags carried in effect force their companions to purchase and pay for those residual caddie services. Many a rider is happy to receive all the tending and tidying. But if you are grouped with an inveterate cart rider who is frugal — and unapproachable to boot — you are well advised to discuss the hiring of the caddie in advance. Before many holes are played, a first-rate caddie will usually find several of the humbug's drives hidden in the deep rough, or otherwise mollify him with helpfulness. However, one misread putt or incorrect distance reading can thwart the relationship for good.

➤ Especially with outgoing caddies, use the first few holes to moderate the amount of conversation and advice to be provided. It may come as a surprise to some, but caddies usually take a personal stake in how well their golfers play. Nevertheless, common sense dictates that any caddie will want you to play well, quickly and also be of good cheer, since these conditions tend to reduce his exertion and increase his pay. In addition, good scores usually reflect the caddie's ability to choose clubs and read the greens.

It sometimes happens that, early in a round, a caddie's blind confidence in a player's ability provides a magical boost that inspires good play for the entire round. If the player is not used to taking caddies, he runs the risk of showing unbounded appreciation, thus uncorking the caddie's entire repertoire of strategy pointers, swing theory and philosophy of life. By about the 11th or 12th holes, someone in the group will become irritated by this sideshow, and usually with good reason. If you want to restrain your caddie's monologues in a non-reproving way, do it early in the round.

➤ On specifics such as reading greens and selecting clubs, establish a quick phrase that squelches all advice. Terse statements such as "I like my read," or "I've got the club" should prevent the caddie's own notions from interrupting your flow at those instinctive moments when you, the golfer, know just what to do.

➤ With a less experienced caddie, you won't be troubled by unwanted advice, but you may feel poorly served, even burdened. No sooner was caddying invented than complaints about lousy caddies were first raised. If you take caddies all the time, you are going to have some dull-witted ones. Your only recourse is, at your club, to get involved with the recruitment and training and, at a resort or public course, to call ahead and state your clear desire to have one of the better caddies assigned to you.

ADDITIONAL CONSIDERATIONS
FOR THE CADDIE TAKER

➤ At courses with large numbers of caddies, it is the responsibility of the caddie to keep his group moving. If your foursome holds up play all day, you may not mind, but the caddies in the group will definitely take some heat when they get back in. Other transgressions by the players, such as driving carts in forbidden spots and hitting before the group ahead is out of range, will result in reprimands to the caddies. Yet another reason to uphold your responsibilities and observe proper course etiquette.

➤ Stowing cash and valuables in your bag at any time is risky. When you have hired a caddie, it presents a particular problem: Despite the fact that there are opportunities for other hands to slip into the appropriate pockets of that golf bag, the caddie assigned to you will be universally seen as guilty. If he is guilty, that's one thing. If he isn't, and didn't even know your valuables were in the bag he was carrying, you could find that you have played an unwitting role in ruining the caddie's reputation.

➤ When you and the other player sharing your caddie hit shots to opposite sides of the fairway, one of you will either have to take an assortment of clubs and walk alone to his ball, or wait patiently for the caddie to cross back over.

➤ In the rain, the best arrangement is for the caddie and the players to each have umbrellas. If there aren't enough to go around, the caddie will do without, holding his players' umbrellas while they play and keeping the clubs as dry as possible using towels and rainhoods. The steel ribs of the umbrella, by the way, serve as a pretty fair "clothesline" for drying gloves and small towels.

➤ A novice caddie may be so ignorant of the Rules of Golf that he or she would be capable of tending a pin while you putt then failing to remove it in time. Your ball hits the flagstick (or the caddie or a towel he may have dropped) and trouble begins. In match play, you have lost the hole; in stroke play, you are penalized two strokes and must play the deflected ball from where it comes to rest. This is perhaps the most obvious infraction among the many you can suffer due to a caddie's error.

➤ Avoid removing and replacing clubs in the golf bag while the caddie has it on his shoulder; it is awkward and uncomfortable for the caddie, and seldom necessary. Hand the club to the caddie if he is walking, or wait until the bag is down.

➤ At halfway houses and beverage carts, it is expected the players will buy the caddies whatever snacks, beverages etc. they may need.

➤ At the end of the round, the caddie should indicate to the player that all the clubs are accounted for and wiped clean.

At its highest peaks — the pro tours — and its deepest roots — Scotland's fabled links — golf with a caddie along as your guide, witness and conscience is the natural thing. Seen in that light, there must be something to it.

C H A P T E R

I X

Making a Match

*It helps to know the protocol,
as well as the pro to call*

For a game that requires no human opponent and is played over lonely hills or through quiet forests, golf is hardly a solitary experience. At public courses, we are bundled into units of four in order to increase volume and thereby help the facility pay its vendors each month. Private clubs, meanwhile, screen and initiate their members with care, thus assuring themselves that fellowship will abound within the ranks. On this basis, it would be odd for a member to *not* want company when he plays, wouldn't it?

Of course, when the club initiation system breaks down, the results are fairly bleak. There are more than a few cases of dues-paying newcomers failing to form the bonds that make showing up for golf an easy, natural thing. Often, when the club represents a higher rung on the social ladder, a new member can run a fairly high risk of finding himself seated alone on the veranda on a

Sunday morning, pining for the warm old days at Scruffy Valley.

When it works, the club system creates a happy roster of keen, congenial golfers. And no book of advice for easing relations among them could ever supplant the folkways and rituals that all regular foursomes eventually establish. Shady Creek's 8:26 group of Perry-Kosco-Taggert-Green, on the tee every weekend morning for the past 12 years, would sooner drink absinthe with their morning donuts than take counsel from a book such as this. The four have been together so long they either know — second nature — how never to offend or ruffle one another, or (more likely) they are each so resigned to the others' irksome ways they no longer notice them.

But if retirement, job changes and bursitis contrive to disconnect their quadrilateral bond, the scattered individuals would each face an imposing challenge. Not only would they have to sensitize themselves to the quirks, patterns and peeves of new people with whom they would be playing, they would be forced to reveal their inner selves through an act that can be even more telling than one's on-course behavior; namely, the choosing of companions.

There being such a dissimilarity in the nature of match-making between club golfers and public links players, it seems best to discuss the procedures on each side separately. As with the foursomes of long standing whose members tolerate each others' warty behavior, a pair of public-golf buddies who play a late-afternoon nine together on a little course in the cornfields needs no help arranging to play. But for publinxers in this age of pumped-up popularity for golf, the instinctive "Let's play golf" too often translates to: "Let's move heaven and earth trying to get a tee time, then see who's available to play." In areas that are particularly underserved with courses, avid players regularly find themselves securing tee reservations first, then dipping into their pool of usual mates to pencil in the names.

Within one of these task forces of a half dozen or a dozen golfers, it is common for several to be at work booking tee reservations at different courses for the coming weekend. The process tends to go like this: Steve is trying to get two tee times at Twin Brook; if he can, then Joe and Joe's brother will make one foursome with Kelly and Chris, and Bob and Rick and Steve will make the other foursome with either Jonesy or Paul. If that doesn't work out, Steve and Chris want to drive up to Blue Lake, ...etc.

Under these conditions, an every-golfer-for-himself mode sometimes prevails. When the day comes to play, who gets onto the course may be unclear, and someone may have to drop out. To reduce the likelihood of hurt feelings, it is up to all involved to observe certain conventions:

➢ Whoever did the work to nail down the elusive reservation not only takes a spot, but also gets to hold one other spot for his or her closest golf buddy.

➢ If there is a cookout, card game or other post-golf party, those who have set it up get to go off the tee first, no questions asked.

➤ In the event of a six-golfers-for-four-spots squeeze play, consideration should be given to players who withdrew stoically last time this happened, or who dropped everything to fill out a foursome on late notice when they were asked.

➤ When players state their interest in playing on a given day with certain other golfers, they ought not to make a major issue out of which course the tee time eventually ends up at. Unless one of the courses under consideration is unusually expensive, casting one's lot in with the group shouldn't be conditioned on the eventual site.

➤ If the group expects to function as a flexible, floating public golf party, each member must be mindful that there will be disappointments along the way, and accept their fate accordingly.

With the USGA handicap system now so developed, a competitive, well-balanced match can be staged among four golfers who have never seen one another before. In public golf, this advantage makes quite a difference to players who yearn to compete. To those who play for other reasons, securing an official USGA handicap, decimal points and all, may not justify the time and money it requires. Without taking up the argument some would make that only people with official handicaps can be "real golfers," we would say merely that having one makes it easier, in certain instances, to get a game. Call the USGA handicap line at 1-908-234-2300 to find out what's involved. In most cases, just playing a minimum number of witnessed rounds per season is all you need.

Competitiveness and the inclination to wager are key points of difference among golfers. Anyone contemplating a golf date with someone they've never played with before should be certain to broach the topic of betting and competing.

A final point regarding compatablity of public links golfers is perhaps the most important. It is a universal rule requiring all golfers at all times to be pleased and eager to play with whomever they are grouped with by the starter. If you are concerned that you are not competent to play with accomplished players, tell the starter.

Whatever it takes, become one of those people who can be paired with anyone in the world and be able, based on a common love for the game, to make a new friendship. If you don't, you miss the essence of golf.

Compatability is, in some respects, handled differently in the club golf setting where making a match is complicated by social boundaries and formalities, rather than problems of access. If you are about to join a club, here are the factors that will influence your adeptness or lack thereof at finding an ongoing source of golf companions:

➢ The people who sponsor you will have to play with you, at least sometimes.

➢ You will play with family and invited guests, and perhaps make more casual, non-prime time golf dates that lead up to that vaunted, weekend-morning appearance.

➤ You will find other new members in your same position.

➤ The golf professional and staff will sometimes be effective in matching you up with compatible people.

➤ Tournaments. You may enter as a single and be drawn as a partner.

➤ Failing all the above, you will quit and go to another club. This has happened in the past and will surely happen again.

IF YOU DON'T LIKE THE WEATHER

Truly adverse weather, especially cold or wet conditions, usually creates an especially strong bond of togetherness among golfers. It's a nice experience, if you can handle it.

But some people just cannot seem to latch on to the concept that "it never rains on the golf course," or, Scottish style, "If it's nae wind and nae rain, it's nae golf." To avoid any misunderstanding between yourself and a potential playing partner, make a point of bringing up the weather issue when you make a golf date, especially one for a distant time. If chilly weather can be expected but you are so starved for golf you would play on a glacier, it's best to let others know. By not bringing it up, you put them in what they may consider to be the awkward position of scratching on game day even though others stick to the plan and head out amid snowflakes. By giving someone an advance opportunity to say, "I don't enjoy playing in temperatures under 50 degrees," you allow them to bow out with some dignity.

In wet weather, the decision to play or not play can be greatly influenced by whether the parties involved prefer to walk or take carts. During and after soaking rains, many courses refuse to allow motorized carts on the course. For golfers who've grown dependent on four-wheel transportation, the issue of the day may be the walking, not the raindrops. You are always better off stating beforehand whether you relish or run from the prospect of playing on foot.

In parts of the country that experience both extremes of temperature, there is less dishonor in bowing out of a scheduled golf date on extremely hot, humid days than under cold, wet conditions. Apparently, even the proudest stoics find little to love about sauna-bath weather. In any case, it is poor manners for the frost lovers to condemn their less hardy brethren. The less hardy, meanwhile, should remember that golf is an outdoor sport and opportunities to play do not come easily. With the advancements in outerwear fiber technology, you can be reasonably comfortable in bad weather and still have the course to yourselves.

C H A P T E R

X

The Friendly Rule Book

*You should know the book, but
never throw it at anyone*

According to dinner-table etiquette, elusive foods such as peas or diced carrots may be nudged onto one's fork with the help of a certain implement. Obviously, the implement in question is not one's thumb, nor is it one's knife. The permitted device is a piece of bread. This is an obscure bit of information that hardly applies to most of our dining experiences. However, in instances when one dines in company where genteel manners are necessary, it would be a handy thing to know.

Similarly, when entering a sand bunker during a round of golf, it is proper to carry along a rake and permissible to drop it alongside the ball. However, according to Rule 13-4 of the official Rules of Golf, it is a two-stroke penalty (or, in match play, loss of hole) to rake any footprints or other disturbances before playing your shot. Respect for the golf course and your desire to avoid delay notwithstanding, that quick pass of the rake provides you with a free test of the sand's consistency, and that's an unfair tactic, according to the rules makers.

Complete adherence to the entire codified Rules of Golf is, of course, seldom called for. In a world of mulligans, preferred lies, and gimme putts, to invoke the official Rules on every shot of every friendly round would be considered a sign of flinty malcontentedness. Because the Rules are so difficult to master, most golfers assume that a person's sole motive for learning them is to nitpick the afternoon away, destroying all sense of enjoyment.

The fact is, knowing the rules does not automatically turn a person into an officious prig, and it is uncharitable to assume that it would. Plenty of rules-savvy golfers bow to unofficial custom when it comes to popular conventions such as mulligans (free take-over of the first tee shot), balls lost in fallen autumn leaves (allowing a free drop instead of calling for a one-stroke penalty and return to the spot played from) and the carrying of more than 14 clubs. They don't wish to turn a casual match into the U.S. Open, even though they pride themselves on knowing the rules by which a U.S. Open is conducted. Actually, what they are likely to do is discuss the most popular local rules before play begins, thus warding off confusion and misunderstanding.

The point of this chapter is not to equate rules ignorance with inferiority or outlaw behavior. The point is to show that knowledge of the Rules, when paired with a practical, compassionate sense of when to invoke or waive them, affords a golfer the widest possible opportunity for helping himself and others enjoy the day's game. People make the mistake of seeing the Rules as an institution that never wants to giveth and always wants to taketh away. Therefore, they dismiss the possibility of warmth in a golfer who knows the rule book cold. Expertise and liberalism need not, however, conflict. In fact, what golf's rules makers probably should do is print up two rule books: the present one, covering every situation and listing all penalties and all reprieves; and a slimmer, completely pardoning version, in which only the unpunished, allowable little acts and mistakes are catalogued.

The following list is by no mean a complete inventory of golf's forgiven sins, but it describes enough of them to show that rules knowledge, selectively applied, can make you a more charitable, reassuring companion on the links.

RULES THAT GRANT RELIEF AND SUBTRACT STROKES

For the purposes of this listing, picture yourself in a foursome with two relative beginners and one veteran golfer who, despite never having read a rule book, is quick to notify the others of their infractions and penalties, whether or not any occurred. As one who knows the Rules, you are able to dismiss this person's mean-spirited, incorrect declarations. Thus, you prevent the two newcomers from forming an image of golf as an even harsher and more penal game than it already is.

➤ From its teed-up position, the ball is nudged to the ground by the club, blown off by the wind or just falls off. Count no stroke, simply re-tee and play. Rule 11-3 states that, on the tee, a player must be moving the club forward with intent to strike the ball for a stroke to be counted. (Once out on the hole, your ball is considered to be "in play," meaning that if it moves after address it must be replaced and a penalty stroke counted. Only, however, if it moves and comes to rest in a new place — merely jostling a ball does not cost you a stroke.)

➤ Someone accidentally drives a golf cart over their putter and bends the shaft. They are told it is against the rules to either straighten the shaft or to play with it in a bent condition. This is false. Rule 4-2 allows either option. Rule 4-4 even permits replacement of a damaged club during the round. (Not if the damage results from a temper tantrum, however). Oh yes, in match play when a player runs over his or his partner's ball with a cart, the Rules say: play it. Most people would allow you to lift and drop it, though.

➤ A player preparing to try a 15-foot side-hill putt asks his partner how much break should be played. The partner looks the situation over then leans down to point out a dark patch of grass about halfway to the hole, declaring this the spot to play for. Someone protests, calling this a two-stroke penalty. They are wrong. It would only be a penalty if the partner had touched the line of the putt with his hand or some object.

➤ A player from the team that has just lost the honor plays first off the tee, anyway. An opponent declares this out-of-turn player's drive invalid and informs the player that he will have to play a new drive in his proper turn and add a penalty stroke to his score. A glance at Rule 10-1 contradicts this claim. The mistaken player does have to wait his turn and play a new ball, but he is not assessed a penalty stroke.

➤ A player and his partner hit into the same bunker. One of them steps into the bunker and mistakenly hits his partner's ball out. An opponent tells them they have lost the hole for hitting a wrong ball. Rule 15-2 says they have lost nothing. If you make this mistake in a hazard, you merely replace the ball and play the correct one. No strokes counted, no penalty.

➤ Just as he is about to putt, a player notices a ball-mark several inches from his ball and decides to repair it. In doing so, he accidentally moves his ball. He is told that this counts a stroke. Not so. Proper procedure is to replace the ball as near as possible to its original position and finish the hole.

➤ A drive comes to rest in a part of the fairway marked ground-under-repair, so the golfer who hit this ball picks it up and drops it one club length behind the marked area. After it lands, the ball rolls several feet and hits the player's golf bag. According to his opponent, this is a breach of Rule 19-2, resulting in loss of the hole. Actually, the scenario is governed by Rule 20-2, in which the player re-drops without penalty.

➤ A player's 15-foot putt for a score of 3 reaches the edge of the cup and stops, over-hanging the hole. The player can't imagine why it doesn't drop, and stands over it for the full 10 seconds the rules permit. Unaware of the requirement in Rule 16-2 that he tap in after allowing 10 seconds, he waits another 15 seconds, at which point the putt falls. His opponents insist that, with a penalty stroke, his score for the hole is 5. They are wrong. The rule does set 10 seconds (following the player's unde-layed arrival at the hole) as a limit, but it still considers the ball to have been holed by the player's last stroke, and then adds one penalty stroke for the delay. In this case, the total would be 4.

➤ Misjudging the distance to the green on the 5th hole, a player hits a shot very long and to the left. His ball comes to rest on the green for the 11th hole, which is separated from No. 5 green by 25 yards of heavy rough and small shrubbery. His opponent informs him that he must either putt off the 11th green to a place from which he can pitch on to No. 5 green, or lift and drop on such an area, incurring a penalty of one stroke. In reality, the Rules (25-3) do call for the latter procedure, but there is no penalty stroke involved.

➤ A player and his partner each have six-foot birdie putts to win the hole from their opponents. Their balls lie about a foot apart, and each is marked with a dime. One player replaces his ball and sinks the putt. Then it is realized that he replaced his ball on his partner's mark, and is therefore disqualified from the hole under Rule 20-7. The opponents then claim that this infraction disqualifies both partners and awards them, the opponents, the hole. Wrong. Rule 30-3 exculpates the partner who hasn't putted yet.

In each of these examples, the rules makers reveal their intention to forgive innocent mistakes whenever the snafu they create can be reversed. By understanding the quality of mercy within the usually exacting Rules of Golf, a knowledgeable golfer is able to reassure his fellow players in a way that many an ignorant, though predatory, opponent would not understand.

In the few formal settings that still remain in our society, the golf course being, at times, one of them, it is to our advantage to know about the old forms and rules that prevail. With so few people around who still recognize formality in any setting, he or she who does the proper, formal thing when it is called for, will generate not just appreciation, but astonishment.

CHAPTER

XI

Handling Special Situations

The art of soldiering along through adversity

The swing you learn in a typical golf lesson works best from a fair lie on level ground with a wide open target. Translating those techniques to the myriad situations out on the golf course is where golf artistry comes in. Likewise with manners. What you learn about proper behavior usually pertains to normal situations on a sunny day at the country club. However, not every golf day is normal, even if it starts off that way. Here are some options for handling difficult circumstances that can arise at any time.

UNBEARABLY SLOW PLAY

There are many causes and sub-causes of slow play, but the indisputable cause of Slowest Play is severe overcrowding. You can send speedy golfers out onto the world's simplest, most wide open course, and if you send enough of them, at tight enough intervals, they will eventually become backed up. In normal-to-heavy play, in which backups are probably due to a foursome or two becoming temporarily muddled or to the golf course having a particularly difficult sequence of holes, the standard procedure is to endure the problem until the pace of play picks up again.

True gridlock caused by rampant overcrowding is different. Under these conditions, your group is likely to consider walking off and asking for some kind of refund or rain check. Whether you are among those loudly sounding retreat or you are counseling patience, you might do best to make the decision at a point on the golf course from which two or more holes are visible. Better still, flag down a ranger and ask him to give you an honest prognosis. Should group consensus call for walking off, the conversation may turn to strategies for obtaining compensation from the management. One thought to consider: By taking your group's log out of the logjam, you may have helped the facility avoid still further complaints. Also, if you are the only member of a riding foursome who wants to quit, be willing to walk in. Three golfers still need two carts.

This solution isn't available if some members of the foursome elect to stay. In determining a group definition of what is bearable or unbearable, the line might best be drawn at about five-and-a-quarter or five-and-a-half hours. To some people, anything over five hours isn't golf. One special point about these situations: There's usually a preset difference in viewpoint between those who have played a lot of golf recently and those who've gone weeks and weeks without playing. So be honest. Instead of mouthing profundities, admit that your vote is the result of how much you've played or not played lately.

If you opt to stay, don't stay and fight. Some people, when they realize that the group just ahead is not keeping pace, become tempted to "push those guys a little." Translation: Hit when they are barely out of range. In the world of golf course etiquette, this is a high crime, an act of sheer madness. Not only could it cause severe injury, it doesn't speed people up. If anything, it slows them down.

A CHANGE IN THE WEATHER

In Chapter IX, which focuses on arrangements to play, the issue of compatibility between fair-weather and all-weather golfers was examined in detail. Unfortunately, the issue is not laid to rest once the group leaves No. 1 tee.

Changeable weather can quickly threaten a foursome's otherwise firm resolve to see the game through. As stated before, the best way to prevent disappointment and fallout is for the players to state beforehand what their basic attitude is toward playing in the elements.

They should also make clear before starting how wagers will be settled if the round is not completed. A reasonable practice would be to pay off on the nine-hole results, if you get that far, in the round.

Along with making others aware of your willingness or unwillingness to stay out in the rain or heat or cold, you do owe it to the group and yourself to bring some semblance of protective gear on questionable days.

In all discussions of weather and when to quit, the one critical absolute is lightning. Following tragic deaths by electrocution at not one but two major golf championships in 1991, awareness of the peril from electrical storms is especially high. A national data center recently reported that five percent of all deaths by lightning happened on a golf course. It goes beyond improper etiquette, to the realm of the harebrained, to ever question a fellow golfer's retreat from even the hint of a lightning storm.

PLAYING WITH CHILDREN

Outside of safety concerns, the most appropriate instance of golfers leaving the course mid-round is when the group involves a young child who becomes bored and wants to do something else. There is plenty of time in life for a youngster to become addicted to golf, and a love of the game is not something that can or should be force-fed. While an adult beginner ought to be enough of a realist to know in advance how much frustration he or she can bear, a child can't be held accountable for insisting on playing a full round, then wearying of golf after five or six holes and asking to go home. When you bring any raw beginner along, you may want to have a contingency plan should they throw in the towel early.

ETIQUETTE ON THE PRACTICE RANGE

The underprivileged who started out on courses with no driving ranges may never get over the miraculous feeling of spilling out a basket of decent golf balls and knocking them hither and yon for someone else to retrieve.

Even for golfers who've grown up on them, the allure of ranges is quasi-spiritual. For some, a station on the practice tee is akin to a preferred pew in a quiet church. In a world that provides little for us to truly trust, a reliable golf swing is a friend, indeed. The practice range being the only place to groove that trustworthy swing, it's no wonder that people are easily vexed out there. To assure your status as a good citizen among the striped-ball set, follow these guidelines:

➢ If the range is at all crowded, only you and your ball supply should occupy linear space. Clubs, jacket, soft drinks and practice aids you aren't using should be behind you somewhere.

➢ Always hit from the area designated by markers or ropes. If ropes are used, be careful to leave enough room between the ball and the rope. Clubs and wrists have been known to break when balls are played too closely to the rope.

➢ A proper practice session is unhurried and allows for analysis and experimentation. That analytical golfer who makes you wait for a spot on the range is going through the mechanical tinkering that allows her or him to play without delay on the golf course (whether they fulfill that side of the bargain is another question). The point is, no reasonable person can expect another to rush through their bucket of practice balls.

➢ On the other hand, delays of any other nature can't be tolerated, unless the practice area is quite deserted. No chit-chat, no long walks to buy refreshments (do it before), no lengthy time-outs to coach friends.

➢ In fact, loud discussions of swingology between range buddies is unfair to others within earshot. Make your voices audible to each other only.

➢ Offering to move over a station or two so that a pair of practice mates can be next to one another is common sense as well as common courtesy. If these two do make a practice of reporting each other's reverse pivots and incomplete shoulder turns to each other, it's best for all concerned that they not do it long distance.

➢ When a professional is nearby giving a lesson, inadvertent eavesdropping is acceptable, but an obvious, concerted effort to take the same lesson someone else is paying for is quite bad form. Moreover, it could foul up your swing even more, if what's being prescribed doesn't apply to your problems.

➢ On natural grass ranges, it's common for clumps of dirt from one practicer's 7-iron to drift off the clubface and head right into the next practicer's face. This is a difficult problem to solve, because it so seldom occurs repeatedly. If soil texture and wind conditions conspire to cause several successive swings of yours to spritz dirt into your neighbor's eye, courtesy demands that you either move to a new spot or start teeing up some driver shots.

➢ Except at the most obsequious resorts, clean up your station of broken tees, soda cans, empty ball baskets, etc.

ETIQUETTE ODDS AND ENDS

➢ Scorekeeping: A minority of golfers seems to enjoy "keeping the card," and those who enjoy it probably do the best job. When the card is clamped on a golf cart steering wheel on a calm, dry day, writing down 72 numbers correctly is not so difficult for anyone, especially when there are slight delays on most tees.

But if you are walking, and play is proceeding without delay, and wet or windy weather makes it imperative to keep the card pocketed as much as possible, keeping score is damned difficult. Moral of the story: Don't make the scorecard keeper ask you for your score every time, whereupon you begin counting on your fingers. Watch for him or her to pull out the card, then report your score accurately and have it done with.

➤ Picking up mislaid items: Part of being a thoughtful golfer involves scanning the green area for wedges and 8-irons that our mates have used at greenside, then left behind. Likewise with headcovers left on the tee by the group ahead. If you pick up a club or headcover that doesn't belong to your foursome, most golfers would expect you to bring it in to the clubhouse the next time you pass through.

➤ Heeding nature's call on the course: For male golfers, there are times when slicing a ball deep into the woods carries consolation. On golf courses where the woods are not lovely, dark and deep, as the poet wrote, etiquette may demand that we wait for the appearance of a modern comfort station, either on the course or back at the clubhouse.

➤ Jumping off the back tees when No. 1 has a wait: Next time you're on hand for the practice rounds of a PGA Tour event, stand on No. 10 tee in the afternoon and watch the pros snarl at one another for cutting in. The policing of a tour course on Mondays and Tuesdays is left to the player, inevitably leading to hard feelings when a group that only wants to play the back nine tries to slip between groups who started on No. 1 in the morning and are making the turn. Lucky for us amateurs, there is a professional staff with vested authority to allow us off tees other than No. 1 or not allow us, depending on the circumstances.

Where Golf Meets Business

*In the most social of games, commercial
needn't mean crass*

In another time, men of privilege grew business relationships from the fertile soil of prepschool friendship. Their golf clubs were playgrounds where the right people grew up together and became socially bonded customers and clients of one another. That old order has faded, but one principle still holds: The most productive, valuable business-golf experiences are the ones blessed by an atmosphere of pure sociability — just a few old friends having a match.

Today, when real people who play golf mix business with their favorite sport, they usually make no deals on the course. Smart executives tee it up with their clients and colleagues to build relationships and dispense a perk. Specific proposals and hard selling are saved for later.

The reason a golf course is seldom used for concrete deal making is simple:

The experience is supposed to be fun, and hardcore business talk would cut into the fun. The second reason, more subtle and probably more important, is that true golfers want to find out how their business associates conduct themselves on the links and what kind of relationship they feel toward the game.

Of course, you should always be prepared for the exception that proves the rule. Translation: If your customer insists on discussing a deal and reaching some agreement before the 18th hole, it's unlikely he is merely baiting you into a breach of the unwritten rules. The advice here is, make the deal. If you insist on withholding your sales pitch until some more appropriate time, you will risk being thought a prig. And a prig with one fewer commission, at that.

How To Make Best Use Of An Outing

Another change in the landscape of business golf is the booming popularity of the large outing. These jamborees of 40 to 80 or more players are an attempt, using old reliable golf, to establish intimacy on a wholesale basis. But the logistics and the geography pose certain obstacles. As an individual member of the field, you will find it difficult to make many connections on the golf course. You may be best off showing up with a smile that befits any day out of the office. If you are lucky, the party or dinner afterward will offer sufficient opportunity for working the crowd.

The competitive format for these events is usually a Captain's Choice, or Scramble, in which foursomes continually hit from wherever the group's best shot just landed and then discard the three weakest shots from the next volley. Real golf it is not, but somehow competitive zeal often flourishes in a scramble tournament.

Amid the camaraderie and joviality that scrambles generally engender, someone has to take responsibility for the few regulation procedures required of your group. For example, if all the carts are to ride out caravan-style for a shotgun (simultaneous) start, you should take a moment to get proper directions to the hole your group begins on. Also, double-check which set of tees the field is to use and how many tee shots at minimum each player must contribute. Many a shotgun-start tournament has been marred by confusion on these points.

Another common mishap occurs when the group assembles for its four chances at a 10-foot birdie putt. The first player misses by a few inches, walks up and taps in. Under scramble rules, the ball is officially holed out, the group must take par and three chances for birdie go to waste.

Usually, a sheet of rules is attached to each scorecard to guide you through these rules and instructions.

As these examples show, business-related golf outings call upon knowledgeable golfers to provide helpful advice to new initiates. If you are serious about wanting to see golf courtesy and etiquette prevail, there will be times when you have to graciously teach its lessons.

The Company Outing, you may have discovered, is a different animal. In this kin-only scenario, your knowledge of your own corporation's culture is more valuable to you than any outside words of advice, though one suggestion seems worthwhile: Do whatever you do during the day with an eye toward making a humorous or sentimental contribution to the awards ceremony that night. Compared to the golf, which by its nature scatters the participants, the awards dinner is a unifier that usually yields the fondest memories. Keep an eye out for anecdotes.

Between these two extremes, there lies the general run of business-golf experience. Most of the precepts to adhere to in these situations also apply to social golf. Here are a few thoughts:

DOS AND DON'TS OF BUSINESS GOLF

➤ Less experienced golfers sometimes make the mistake of repeatedly tossing out idle suggestions of a golf date to business associates who also play. Between two people who aren't committed to the game, this is a harmless ritual, but it can be irritating to a devotee. When you say, "Oh we must play golf" to a veteran golfer, you should mean it.

➤ Whatever its faults, the golf cart is truly a vehicle for personal bonding. When a foursome is made up of two players from one company and two from another, it is a nice gesture to switch bags at the turn, so that each Company X player rides with each Company Y player for nine holes.

➢ Gift giving can be a fine adjunct to the business-golf experience. Keep in mind, however, that today's golfer is particular about the ball he plays. It's possible to select a $30 dozen of a brand that, given a choice, your recipient would not want to tee up. Another gift problem to avoid involves items that carry the traditional crest of a private club. Some people are uncomfortable wearing a shirt or cap that seems to denote membership in a club.

➢ The mere fact that you are playing client golf in no way grants broad license to bring equipment such as cellular telephones onto the course. If it's really The Big Call that you are waiting for, why are you playing golf? Obviously, health crises and similar matters of urgency may provide a reasonable exception to the no phones rule.

➢ The recent increase in sensitivity toward membership policies affects businesspeople who are invited for golf at private clubs. We are coming to a time when it is the duty of the host to describe the membership make-up of his club before asking a business associate to be his guest there. It may seem awkward, but the possibility of backlash within the guest's corporation — not to mention an affront to her or him personally — is now a fact of life.

CHAPTER

XIII

They Work So You Can Play

It's up to the amateurs to help professionals do their job

No man is a hero to his valet, the saying goes. Likewise, the club golfer who behaves charmingly to his or her peers may show a different shade of personality to the club's professional staff. In general, a person's capacity for warm, productive relations with the facility manager, the golf professional, the greens superintendent and their hired help — or, at least, his ability to meet these people halfway — requires some reflection on daily club life as seen through their eyes.

Start by acknowledging that this employment relationship is a unique one. A golf club member who joins his several hundred peers in retaining a staff of people to direct their recreational activities does no other hiring of this nature in any other facet of his or her life. (The hiring of clergy by a congregation is perhaps the closest parallel). If you work for a corporation or run your own company, you will hire people to work for it, but each of these employees will report only to one boss or to a small team of managers. At a club, every employee reports to every member.

With little to compare themselves to, these golf-club employment relationships must seek their own natural equilibrium. Anyone trying to evaluate how well or poorly a club and one of its key employees were meeting each others' needs would have to refer to the tenure of the previous holder of the job, or else think in terms of the history and tradition of each profession.

For the golf professional, this tradition includes both saints and skeletons. There are stories of 40-year kinships between a club and its revered pro, as well as scandals involving malfeasance and philandering by the pro or dishonesty and capricious firings on the part of the club. More so than most forms of employment, a golf professional's service can soar to heights of heroism or sink into tragic infamy. The amplifying factor, again, is the relatively vast number of bosses/clients that the employee serves, and the intensely personal kinds of services the golf pro administers to his intimate village of families.

Many a club membership has been stunned by its admired professional's departure for a new, apparently equivalent job in the same area; his reason, which they never find out, is that he has looked ahead to what he and many of his peers consider an inevitable falling out between club and pro. By moving to a new job before one of the few members who dislikes his style rises to power, the professional buys what he sees as another half-decade of amicable working conditions. It may seem extreme, but it does happen. And it gives rise to the first of several pieces of general advice for the club member who wishes to contribute to the stability and quality of his club's golf program by promoting positive working relations with the professional staff:

➤ Don't be naive about the pro's political challenge: Like a small-town mayor or a union official, your club pro must avoid even the appearance of favoritism, loose behavior or unsanctioned use of the club's property or its name. What starts as exaggeration for the sake of teasing or humor can come out the other end of the grapevine as damaging talk. The atmosphere is not exactly Orwellian, but a faint trace of paranoia on the part of the pro is often excusable and sometimes even advisable. When any clique of members aspires to become the pro's inner circle, the situation inevitably becomes unhealthy for all concerned.

➤ Don't make him or her into a savior: When a new professional is hired, there is usually a swell of optimism that each member's slice will be cured and every tear in the social fabric will be mended. What the incoming pro needs is a warm welcome, not ridiculous expectations.

➤ Try to avoid making casual assumptions (and suggestions) about how the shop should be run. If a club wants to, it can put together a committee to make suggestions about the shop and its operation. Very few

competent professionals would be unrecep-
tive to this kind of input. In fact, only about
one-half of all golf shops are run as conces-
sions by golf pros who assume all risks and
control the profits. What tends to wear
them down over a long summer is the constant flow of advice from the handful of
people who never operated their own bou-
tiques but always wanted to.

➤ The golf professional, unlike the wooden
Indian at the cigar store, is not on the job
all 90 daylight hours of the week. Of all
complaints about their job performance,
this may be the one pros hear most often
and find most frustrating — that so-and-so
member went to find them one day and
they weren't around. There is a certain critical mass of hours per week that any head
pro must be on hand, and it comes to more
hours than most people work.

Beyond that, the ability to delegate
responsibility and provide full services without being present is the mark of a skilled
professional. Imagine that you could work
your own job a potential 90 hours per week
and that 400 people were not only half-
expecting you to but were mentally marking
you present or absent at all times. It would
become frustrating.

If the membership bears these conditions in mind, it has every right to expect
energetic, imaginative and thoughtful service from their golf professional all season
long. For example, a quality golf lesson
should be bookable with no more than a
week's wait, two or three weeks' wait in the
very busiest periods. Repair and return of
broken or defective clubs should be accom-

plished in less than a few weeks, though some companies are much quicker than this and some much slower.

Basic merchandise — solid shirts, shoes in popular colors and sizes, the top-selling golf balls — should rarely, if ever, be out of stock. A special-order book should be next to the cash register with all the pertinent toll-free numbers available at a glance. In lieu of major inventory commitments, the pro and his staff should be masters of the special-order system, with solid working knowledge of whom to call, how much, how soon, etc.

Further, the professional staff's knowledge of the Rules of Golf should be complete. Their understanding of golf history and tradition should be deep enough to indicate respect for it. Their speed and accuracy in scoring and posting tournament results should not be lacking. And, unless the adult members have no interest, there should be ample provision for the introduction of junior members to the game. If the members are enthusiastic about walking their golf course, it is part of the pro's job to recruit and train a caddie corps. Some courses, because of their remoteness, have much less of a pool of potential caddies to draw upon. In general, however, there are more excuses than there is energy put forth in the name of establishing caddie programs.

Beyond these fundamentals, many of today's PGA professionals look to develop special knowledge or skills in a given area, be it teaching, clubfitting, playing competitively, working with juniors, running professional education programs, etc. Ideally, the interests of the membership will match up to the areas in which their pro is most interested and most skilled.

Relations between club members and the club general manager are less personal than those between members and the pro, but they are, at times, no less problematic. As sometimes happens with the golf professional, the club manager can easily become the focal point of a conflict that develops between membership factions.

When the factions differ vehemently as to how the facilities should be used and what standards of quality should be met, the club manager may be hard-pressed to suggest a compromise that proves satisfactory. As a member, your duty of compassion to the club manager may be limited to the realization that, when you tug him in one direction, you are probably setting him up for a return tug in the opposite direction.

Of the three management people at a club, the greens superintendent is the only one whose activities and achievements can be expressed and contained in a tangible physical product. The course's 18 tees, fairways and greens do a superintendent's talking for him and, when they are in perfect shape, he's a hero.

Unfortunately, perfect is a difficult shape for a golf course to stay in. What the superintendent looks for in the way of proper treatment from members is mostly that they try to learn enough about agronomy to legitimize their complaints. Either via the club officers or the golf staff or both, the superintendent should somehow be communicating to members about the soil conditions and the organisms that, at any given time, are posing obstacles to the attainment of ideal turfgrass. In recent years, clubs have instituted seminar nights in which members who are particularly interested in course maintenance can advance their knowledge of how the maintenance program works. If your club doesn't already do this, you might suggest that such a program be started.

Beyond these natural constraints, there are physical and fiscal limits to what a greens crew can do to replicate Masters week at Augusta National on your course. If course conditions are an obsession of yours, you should look through a few of the turfgrass trade magazines and get some idea as to what generation of maintenance equipment your club currently uses. If your club is equipped with the latest and best machines and irrigation systems, perhaps your lofty expectations are justified. If yesterday's technology — tractor-drawn gang mowers instead of triplex hydraulic riding units, hand rakes instead of motorized sand rakers — fills your maintenance barn, maybe you should settle for yesterday's level of course conditioning.

Your Honor

Golf etiquette for a new age

Any attempt to identify and comment upon every possible aspect of interaction during a round of golf will necessarily miss a few spots. This being the case, we resort to well-chosen generalities and hope they cover the point. The most trustworthy generalities concerning golf courtesy would be these few: You do not have to be a great player to be great to play with; planning and awareness are the most important traits of a thoughtful golfer; everyone is guilty of an occasional lapse; and, most importantly, the purpose of golf is enjoyment and relaxation.

Among all games, golf in particular challenges us to keep frustration — which is inevitable — from turning into desperation, which then robs us of our capacity to be sociable. On that epic landscape called the golf course, we compete against and yet alongside one another, gritty in competition but chivalrous throughout. If we work at it.

The work required, as these pages have tried to show, involves a deepening of our understanding of the people we play alongside and the way in which the rhythms of a round modulate human feelings and behavior. Obviously, there are times when a standard act of courtesy should be foregone so that the recipient, having just hit three straight pitch shots into the same pond, can be alone with his suicidal thoughts. Just as the authors of the Rules of Golf update their statutes every few years, and regularly publish a weighty new volume of relevant Decisions on the Rules, so does golfing society alter and amend its estimation of what, exactly, is appropriate behavior. Even at that, we fall far short of consensus as to the exact details.

But our responsibility persists. Whether or not golf continues to be played in a manner that is more selfless than selfish, more controlled than marked by outbursts, more by the official Rules than in defiance of them — these determinations will be ours to make. With the large influx of new players coming into the sport at once, it represents an opportunity for a new theme, or for old themes, rejuvenated, to be stamped upon the culture of golf. It is hoped that the best of both the old and the new values will enforce themselves.

However long you play the game, and however much your skills sharpen or decline, you are always capable of arriving at the course on a given day and conducting yourself in the most thoughtful, well-mannered, winning style ever. That is not the goal most people set for themselves as golfers, but it is a noble one, worth keeping.